System Innovation for Sustainability 2

System Innovation for Sustainability 2

CASE STUDIES IN SUSTAINABLE CONSUMPTION AND PRODUCTION — MOBILITY

EDITED BY THEO GEERKEN AND MADS BORUP

Greenleaf
PUBLISHING

© 2009 Greenleaf Publishing Ltd

Published by Greenleaf Publishing Limited
Aizlewood's Mill
Nursery Street
Sheffield S3 8GG
UK
www.greenleaf-publishing.com

Printed and bound in the UK by Athenaeum Press Ltd, Gateshead, Tyne & Wear.
Printed on paper that is sourced and harvested from sustainable forests and is FSC-accredited.

Cover by LaliAbril.com.

British Library Cataloguing in Publication Data:
    Case studies in sustainable consumption and production :
        mobility. -- (System innovation for sustainability ; v. 2)
        1. Transportation--Environmental aspects.
        2. Transportation--Social aspects. 3. Transportation and
        state.
        I. Series II. Geerken, Theo. III. Borup, Mads.
        388-dc22

    ISBN-13: 9781906093235

Contents

1
Introduction

Theo Geerken and An Vercalsteren
Flemish Institute for Technological Research (VITO), Belgium

Mads Borup
Technical University of Denmark, Department of Management Engineering

Arnold Tukker
Netherlands Organisation for Applied Scientific Research (TNO)

This book summarises the results for the need area 'mobility' developed during the EU funded SCORE! (Sustainable Consumption Research Exchanges) project. SCORE! is a network initiated with EU funding to support the development of the UN 10 Year Framework of Programmes on Sustainable Consumption and Production. The mission of SCORE! is to organise a leading science network that provides input to this Framework. The EU funding for SCORE! ran between 2005 and 2008, engaging 28 institutions, but by the organisation of various major workshops and conferences the project engaged and structured a larger community of several hundred professionals in the EU and beyond.

The SCORE! philosophy assumes that sustainable consumption and production (SCP) structures can be realised only if experts that understand business development, (sustainable) solution design, consumer behaviour and system innovation policy work together in shaping them. Furthermore, it is believed this should be linked with the experience of actors (industry, consumer groups, eco-labelling organisations) in real-life areas of consumption: mobility, agro-food, energy and electronics. These areas are responsible for 70% of the life-cycle environmental impacts of Western societies (Hertwich 2005; Tukker *et al.* 2006). This led to the following approach to the project:

● The first phase of the project (marked by a workshop co-organised with the EEA [European Environment Agency] in Copenhagen in April 2006) aimed to provide a positive confrontation of conceptual insights developed in the four aforementioned science communities (business development, solution design, consumer behaviour, system innovation policy) of how 'radical' change to SCP can be governed and realised. The results of this phase have been published as the first book in this series, *System Innovation for Sustainability 1: Perspectives on Radical Change to Sustainable Consumption and Production* (Tukker *et al.* 2008)

● The second phase put the three consumption areas at centre stage. SCORE! Work Package leaders inventoried cases 'that work' with examples of successful switches to SCP in their field. In a series of conferences and workshops, these cases were analysed on 'implementability', adapted where needed, and policy suggestions were worked out that can support implementation. The results of this phase are published in this book and in two parallel books covering the areas of food and housing/energy-using products (Tischner *et al.* 2009; Lahlou *et al.* 2010)

1.1 Approach to the analysis of sustainable consumption and production for mobility

1.1.1 Working method

1.1.1.1 Scope

At the start of the SCORE! project the need area 'mobility' had to be defined. As the main focus of SCORE! was sustainable consumption, including the potential contribution that consumers and users can make to a more sustainable future, it was decided not to cover the full range of transport of goods and people, but to limit the scope to the transport of persons. So the focus for mobility is on:

● Passenger transport (instead of freight transport)

● Mobility for both private and professional use

- With as typical transport modes cars, trains, buses, airplanes, bicycles but no cargo ships nor trucks

Based on research on available literature on mobility and transport, three clearly unsustainable issues for mobility were identified as a focus in the selection of cases of the work on mobility in SCORE!

- The high and still increasing contribution to global warming

- Increasing levels of congestion

- Slowly decreasing but still high levels of car accidents with injured people or fatalities (WBCSD 2004; Wells 2007)

1.1.1.2 Process

The SCORE! project was a coordinated action within the EU 6th Framework research programme. Such actions aim to exchange and disseminate good practice, and to promote and support the networking and coordination of research and innovation activities. SCORE! is not a research project that tries to do fundamental new research to solve problems with regard to sustainable consumption.

A specific goal was to build up a research community in the field of SCP to include experts in the different science fields and consumption domains. In the context of the SCORE! project, two conferences and three interactive workshops were organised. As indicated, particularly in the second half of the project the focus was on domains such as mobility.

The first major SCORE! conference in November 2006 marked the switch from a general perspective on change management for SCP to a focus on the domains of mobility, food, housing and energy-using products. In the 'mobility' session examples were presented by researchers from universities and non-governmental organisations (NGOs) addressing the following topics:[1]

- The growing intensity of tourism mobility

- The importance of the environmental impacts of transport infrastructure

- High investments in improving the speed of transport with significant environmental consequences

- The role of information and labelling at the 'consumption junction' of buying a new car

---

1 The proceedings of this dedicated mobility session at the SCORE! launch conference are available as part 3 on the SCORE! project website, www.score-network.org, accessed 17 March 2009.

- A scenario analysis of bus and train compared with car (sharing), showing that the use of buses and trains is much cheaper but also much slower for the user

- Innovation diffusion not as a linear process but as a branching process and the hypotheses that successful innovations show self-reinforcing effects as a result of interaction between different and complex feedback loops

- The upcoming trend of personal 'aeromobility'

After this conference, in June 2007, a workshop was organised dedicated to the different domains. Researchers sent in cases that showed either success or failure on the path to sustainable mobility. A case should be more than a good idea and has been defined as an implemented change that can be evaluated in terms of its success or failure. Several criteria were applied in the selection of cases for presentation. They were chosen for wide variety of approach, different mobility modes and European geographical distribution. During the workshop the selected cases were evaluated and the lessons learned reported. Selected, edited cases presented in the mobility session of this workshop have been included as Chapter 3–10 in this book.

For a follow-up workshop in November 2007 the project team prepared 'thought-provoking statements' about the problems and possible solutions in the mobility need area to stimulate the debate. Participants were invited to make them stronger, better or supply counterevidence or add new statements. This resulted in a final list of statements that provide a compact reflection on the problems, trends, windows of opportunity and actions required for the need area 'mobility'. These statements are presented in Boxes 11.1–11.5 in Chapter 11, on mobility, and formed the basis for suggestions for sustainability improvements in that domain.

1.1.2 Contributors and responsibilities

The SCORE! team members from VITO and RISØ were responsible for running the process within the mobility need area, organising the interaction during the workshops, performing desktop research, providing case studies, writing the need area description and concluding chapters.

The SCORE! members of the project contributed by providing and presenting case studies and by active participation during workshop discussions.

Any other participants in this networking project either from the research community, policy circles, industry or NGOs were invited to provide and present cases and actively to participate. We want to thank them all for their input and intense collaboration providing collective insights in the complex field of mobility within SCP.

1.1.2.1 Book outline

In the next chapters, the following points will be discussed:

- Chapter 2 gives a generic analysis of the mobility need area, including sustainability challenges and a general analysis of potential for change

- Chapters 3–10 describe the case studies according to a prestructured analytical format

- Chapter 11 reflects on the findings and conclusions within the area of mobility and provides a link to the general SCP framework

References

Hertwich, E.(2005) 'Life-cycle Approaches to Sustainable Consumption: A Critical Review', *Environmental Science and Technology* 39.13: 4,673.

Lahlou, S., M. Charter and T. Woolman (eds.) (2010) *System Innovation for Sustainability 4: Case Studies in Sustainable Consumption and Production—Housing/Energy-Using Products* (Sheffield, UK: Greenleaf Publishing, forthcoming).

Tischner, U., E. Stø, U. Kjærnes and A. Tukker (eds.) (2009) *System Innovation for Sustainability 3: Case Studies in Sustainable Consumption and Production—Food and Agriculture* (Sheffield, UK: Greenleaf Publishing, forthcoming).

Tukker, A., M. Charter, C. Vezzoli, E. Stø and M. Munch Andersen (eds.) (2008) *System Innovation for Sustainability 1: Perspectives on Radical Change to Sustainable Consumption and Production* (Sheffield, UK: Greenleaf Publishing).

——, G. Huppes, S. Suh, R. Heijungs, J. Guinée, A. de Koning, T. Geerken, B. Jansen, M. van Holderbeke and P. Nielsen (2006) *Environmental Impacts of Products* (Seville, Spain: European Science and Technology Observatory [ESTO]/Institute for Prospective Technological Studies [IPTS]).

WBCSD (World Business Council for Sustainable Development) (2004) 'Mobility 2030: Meeting the Challenges to Sustainability'; www.wbcsd.org/plugins/DocSearch/details.asp?type= DocDet&ObjectId=NjA5N, accessed 17 March 2009.

Wells, P. (2007) 'Deaths and Injuries from Car Accidents: An Intractable Problem?', *Journal of Cleaner Production* 15: 1,116-21.

2
Review of the mobility domain

Theo Geerken

Flemish Institute for Technological Research (VITO), Belgium

An Vercalsteren

Flemish Institute for Technological Research (VITO), Belgium

Mads Borup

Technical University of Denmark, Department of Management Engineering

Mobility and transport are areas that have already been studied intensively in the past from varying angles, resulting in a wide body of available literature. Three recent books that cover the main aspects of the sustainable mobility area from a reviewing and system perspective are worth mention as they provide a basic understanding from similar or complementary angles:

- *The Business of Sustainable Mobility: From Vision to Reality* (Nieuwenhuis *et al.* 2006) is based on a Greening of Industry Network Conference from 2003 and addresses motorised land-based mobility, with a focus on the 'central problem' of the private car. The authors describe radical (system) changes needed for (technological) innovation in the supply chain in the powertrain, new business models and alternative and radical concept vehicles

- *Experimenting for Sustainable Transport: The Approach of Strategic Niche Management* (Hoogma *et al.* 2002) stresses the importance of strategic experiments in nurtured spaces, creating learning experiences and providing intermediary steps towards regime shifts that take long periods of time, changes in social fabric and changes in systems of related techniques

- *Achieving Sustainable Mobility: Everyday and Leisure-time Travel in the EU* (Holden 2007) addresses personal mobility and stresses the important growth in leisure-time travel (including tourism) accounting for 50% of the distances travelled in the developed world. Six hypotheses, also frequently seen as strategies for sustainable transport, about energy chains, public transport, green attitudes and land-use planning are investigated and critically evaluated using empirical data

In our book we focus on changes towards sustainable personal mobility based on implemented cases and desktop research analysed from a system perspective with an explicit role for the user and/or consumer.

2.1 Systemic description of the domain

2.1.1 Introduction: context factors and meta-trends for the mobility domain

The demand for mobility during the past two centuries shows a pattern of continuous growth. Important socioeconomic meta-trends that had and still have an important influence on this total demand for mobility are:

- An increasing population as a result of greater life expectancy. This has made a major contribution to total consumption levels of mobility in the past century. As from around 2005 European population is stabilising and projections foresee a gradual decline in population

- Individualisation. Even though the rate of population growth is decreasing, the number of households is increasing continuously (owing to smaller family sizes, divorces, elderly living longer independently and so on). The number of people per household in the EU-15 fell from 2.8 in 1980 to 2.5 in 2005 (EEA 2005). Each household needs mobility solutions, and the availability of more collective consumption patterns is decreasing

- Increase in double-income households. Participation rates of women in the labour market have increased considerably. As work no longer tends to be located near the home because of a much stronger professional specialisation since the industrial revolution, each worker needs a solution to the commute and between 1995 and 2006 car ownership levels in the EU-27 increased by 22% (EEA 2009)

- Internationalisation and globalisation. The world is developing in the direction of an open international economy. This leads automatically not only to higher volumes of transported goods but also to more business and leisure trips. World trade is growing even faster than the world GDP (OECD 2006). Companies that used to have a strong national basis a century ago now are European or world players with offices and factories all around the world. Owing to the international labour market this drives an increase in business trips, and, indirectly, an increase in leisure trips and expatriate trips. Professional development through knowledge networks is much more pronounced outside one's own company or institution. In many cases the networks are international to a greater or lesser extent

- Urban sprawl. The increasing majority of the population lives in urbanised areas, and many people prefer to live in the outskirts of the bigger cities, leading to urban sprawl. Quite often the development of public transport systems does not hold pace with the rapid development of new residential areas, forcing people into cars to commute. The car is frequently the only practical alternative and there is evidence that this increases travel-related energy consumption in cities when population densities fall (EEA 2006b). Choices in 'spatial planning' have consequences for more (car) mobility needs such as choosing locations of shopping centres or business parks outside the city centre, with sometimes bad connections for public transport, choices to eliminate small town schools and to concentrate education into larger schools and so on

- Increase in welfare combined with available leisure time and the perceived need to enjoy more and more frequent shorter holidays. Available leisure time has increased over the decades, and the demands as well as the budget for more leisure trips abroad have also increased

- The rapid ICT developments of recent decades have created new inspiring opportunities to improve the sustainability performance of mobility systems but have also promoted new needs for (international) mobility in wider networks

For personal travelling there also exists a theory (the Brever law; Hupkes 1982) that during history people have always been willing to travel on average approximately one hour per day and will try to reach further destinations when the technical and economical possibilities arise to travel faster. An associated explanation is that humans behave like a territorial animal, always trying to expand its territory. The faster the transport modes, the greater the distances travelled (for users with no time or budget constraints). As mobility realised through cars or airplanes is among the highest-scoring energy-using human activities per unit of time (Jalas 2002) the consequences for environmental emissions are significant. The example of the introduction of the French network of high-speed rail (TGV) also shows the 'law of growing demand' as it not only induced some modal shift from air to rail but also created extra demand (EEA 2006a).

2.1.2 The mobility 'landscape': system specifics

The provision of mobility infrastructure has always been considered an important task for national states and other public authorities. Most of the time, the focus in this challenge has been on establishing and developing an infrastructure that enables people to move from one place to another and to do it faster than previously possible. Greater speed, longer distances and accessibility have been key issues. Even the production of vehicles (especially cars and airplanes) has for a long time been a state-supported activity because of national interests, although in recent years the free market with fair competition rules is taking over the rules of the game. An example of an attempt (with limited success so far) to create freer market mechanisms in public transport is the splitting up of railway companies. In this system, a public state-owned company provides infrastructure maintenance and development, with another company operating the trains and services, simultaneously opening up the market for other private companies to provide competing services.

A number of engineering communities have been heavily involved in the technological progress of vehicle technology that for many years was focused on reliability improvement, safety and cost price.

Institutions in the mobility area have for many years been created with the aim of extending and improving the infrastructure as much as possible, without much attention to other issues. This, for example, is the case with road agencies in a number of countries.

For a long period this was the prevailing aim, with no other perspective to challenge it at a fundamental level. There has been no 'cap' on the challenge of increasing the distances and speed achievable. In most recent years, this situation has changed and some serious challenges to the very essence of the prevailing perspective have appeared. It is now the understanding that mobility infrastructure is not always only a public good but can also contribute to significant problems in society.

Globalisation is the extreme result of this tendency, but at the same time it also a sign of the end of it. It is now usual (in rich parts of the world) for people to be able to travels around the planet. Also, goods are transported all the way around the world, sometimes more than once, to be consumed in a completely different part of the world than that in which they are produced. Now, distance cannot be further extended and a limitation in some sense has been reached, both practically and symbolically.

A characteristic of the current landscape is that international transport is to some extent less regulated than national transport. Among the reasons for this is that international transport is understood as a good and valuable thing and that to some extent it has been out of the reach of planning institutions and regulation. Institutions at the international level are relatively weak compared with those at the national level. In recent years, there has been a development in institutions that can address international transport.

One aspect of this is that fuel for airplanes and ships, which constitutes a major part of the international transport system, have not been subject to the same regulation and taxation as fuel for cars and other modes of transport, which is to a larger extent used in domestic transport. A new political development within the EU climate change policy area seems to be bringing an end to this situation by planning to apply the Emission Trading Scheme to air transport (EU 2008).

2.1.2.1 Socioeconomic trends

Economists have argued that mobility infrastructure is an important prerequisite for economic growth and development for overall society. This becomes evident when looking at the purposes of our mobility behaviour. The main purposes for travel are for commuting, business, education, shopping, leisure and other personal business (such as visiting friends). Statistics on these use patterns can be obtained only by surveys, but these are not carried out every year and are far from being harmonised across Europe. As a consequence, there are no good European statistics. For Great Britain the distribution of trips according to purpose for the period 1999–2001 is shown in Figure 2.1.

Over the years the distribution of purposes for trips has not changed drastically, although travel for leisure is increasing. The total distance travelled nonetheless keeps on rising every year. In the future the statistics on mobility might be improved and be used in activity-based modelling, which provides better insights into the relationships between the needs for and emissions of mobility (Beckx et al. 2009).

The (general) transport sector itself provides over 10 million jobs in the EU and contributes with 7% to GDP but it also accounts for approximately 70% of all oil

FIGURE 2.1 Trips per purpose in Great Britain, 1999–2001

Source: UK Department of Transport 2006

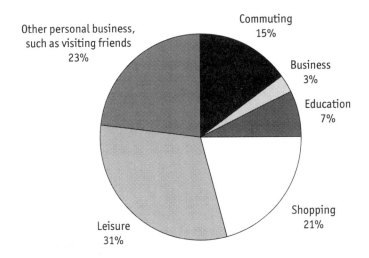

consumption (EU 2006) and 20–40% of basic materials such as cement, steel and aluminium for infrastructure and vehicles (Holden 2007).

The consequence of all these meta-trends is that the needs and wants associated with mobility have increased and continue to increase. Trade grows even faster than GDP owing to globalisation, and as a consequence both passenger and freight transport grow at a faster rate than GDP.

Another consequence of these trends is that the need for mobility is deeply embedded in society, and that society has been built around mobility. Mobility cannot easily be reduced because of various 'lock-in' situations. Consumers and professionals, among others, can become locked in to their mobility needs for economic, social and professional reasons.

2.1.2.2 Specific political developments

Transport policy has for decades been an issue for each nation separately. Liberalisation started in the 1980s, and the number of regulatory regimes with a market focus started to rise. This has meant that there has been a move away from a picture of transport and mobility as something that could be handled and run by public authorities and institutions to something that runs itself through the choices of many individuals and which only to a limited extent should be supported and managed by policy-makers and public institutions. In practice, there are, however, still considerable public efforts (investments, support) in the mobility area, although public funding is lacking in general. Owing to the 'headache of funding' Europe has promoted so-called public–private partnerships since the end of the 20th century (EU 2001). In many countries there has been a tendency towards the privatisation of the public institutions that run public transport systems. This combination of liberalisation and market focus is connected to the general tendency towards individualisation, including in mobility.

It is only since December 1992 that European efforts started to become more integrated, with the publication of a white paper (EU 1992). Efforts were directed towards opening up a single European market with a 'level playing field', allowing for fair competition, and a single European 'sky', facilitating the interoperability of public infrastructure for (high-speed) trains and airplanes. Remote areas of Europe were connected through new infrastructure to spread socioeconomic development across Europe and to fulfil the 'assumed' right for personal mobility. This development has succeeded and has led to continuously rising levels of mobility and freight transport.

Regarding environmental policy, the first European requirements were set for emissions per kilometre for personal cars and light trucks in 1993 with the start of the Euro 1 emissions standard. This has proven to be a continuously moving standard, with every change moving towards more stringent targets—and with great success. Currently, the Euro 4 standard applies, and Euro 5 is proposed for 2008–2009.

Decoupling was achieved for polluting emissions such as carbon monoxide (CO), hydrocarbons (HCs), nitrogen oxides (NO_x) and particulates through these emission standards. Absolute decoupling has also been achieved in reducing acidifying emissions thanks to the policy and technical feasibility of lowering the sulphur content of fuels. Lead as a fuel additive and its associated disperse emissions could be abandoned thanks to technical adaptations in the internal combustion engine. Nonetheless, leaded fuel is still used in many countries outside the EU-25 (UNEP/EEA 2007). Harmful emissions have declined in general and in absolute quantity, but air quality problems require continued attention, especially in urban environments (EEA 2007). Despite a voluntary agreement with car producers (the ACEA Covenant [EU 1999]), the carbon dioxide (CO_2) emissions of cars have not reduced significantly because engine efficiency and aerodynamic improvements have been counterbalanced by the increasing weight of cars resulting from the demand for greater levels of comfort and safety. Also, consumer buying behaviour has shifted to bigger and heavier cars despite the availability of smaller cars. The European Commission is now striving for regulation of the CO_2 emissions from cars.

Trains nonetheless showed good progress through the electrification of the railways, which increased overall efficiency and considerably reduced emissions.

Air transport has been historically a special case because national authorities have little to say about flying in international areas. In most countries national air companies have in the past been heavily supported or owned by the state, as there was recognition that this is an important area for good international relations in a globalising world. The very low levels of tax on fuels for air transport are also attributable to this state support. In recent years, nonetheless, the liberalisation of air transport has begun. As a consequence of this policy of opening up the market the so-called low-cost carriers serve the most frequently used destinations first, bringing down the price levels considerably and forcing the other companies to work more efficiently as well. This significant price reduction has increased the affordability of air travel and as consequence has increased the frequency of short holidays ('sun snacks' and city trips) for many people.

Another recent political development is the fact that new players at an intermediate political level have entered the arena in achieving sustainable transport in urban environments. Some 80% of Europeans live in an urban environment, and these inhabitants suffer most from traffic congestion, accidents and pollution. 'Cities themselves, rather than the EU, are in the driving seat' (EU 2006: 14). Cities can develop sustainable transport policies—including, for example, parking policies, improvements to public transport, the creation of bus and car-pooling lanes, congestion charges and limitations on access to certain types of (polluting) cars—but not all measures are straightforward from a legal point of view.

2.1.2.3 Specific sociocultural developments

In many cases lifestyle aspects and fashions play an important role in connection to mobility. For example, the increase in adventure travels and extreme sport is connected to mobility and the freedom that is associated with being able to move to where one wants. The exhibition of wealth is often connected to mobility, not least through the possession of expensive and fast cars, but also through, for example, an increase in the number of people who own houses or apartments in other countries and who several times a year take travels to those homes, or in people that go on weekend trips for shopping in London or Milan, to spend a Saturday in Cairo and so on.

In many European countries an increasing number of people have become economically well-off and rich. Levels of consumption are, to a larger degree than before, determined by fashion and lifestyle issues rather than by basic needs such as for food and a place to live. Evidently, not everybody has the same needs, preferences and (economic) possibilities for mobility, and making generalisations about people's behaviour is dangerous. Neither is it easy to classify mobility users or mobility behaviour into simplified boxes; nonetheless, a helpful classification for mobility types was constructed based on in-depth interviews (Jensen 1999) following the concept of ideal types from the Weber typology:

- The passionate car drivers (6.3%)

- The everyday car drivers (33%)

- The leisure-time car drivers (36.4%)

- The cyclists/public transport users of heart (1.4%)

- The cyclists/public transport users of convenience (16.4%)

- The cyclists/public transport users of necessity (6.5%)

Evidently, people cannot be permanently or uniquely classified into mobility types, and their behaviour varies depending on the goal of the journey in question. Important contextual factors differentiating the mobility types include the location of home and work (urban, rural, etc.), employment status, whether or not there are children in the household and income level. There are also differences regarding distance travelled.

People categorised into the above mobility types were asked about the symbolic meaning of the car for them; 'the car as a symbol of freedom or independence' was the most cited statement. This statement was supported not only by approximately 80% of the car drivers but also by about 55% of the bikers/public transport users. Remarkably, 'the car emphasises one's personality' and 'the car as a symbol of status' received support from less than 20% of car drivers and bikers/public transport drivers. This most probably reflects the difference or gap between stated preferences and real preferences. We all know that the type of car, like clothing, creates symbolic value for the owner or driver. The same applies to our choice of holiday destination or choice of frequency of short vacations. Apart from creating some relief from stressful daily activities, it also contributes to our status or image in society.

Air transport has developed over time from heroism and progress at the early stage of development (Rispens 2003) to, today, an enabler for globalisation and cultural exchanges on a world scale.

Another important sociocultural development is the decreasing level of acceptance of nuisance (pollution and noise) from transport by people living close to roads and airports. It is also becoming clearer that our collective behaviour leading to higher levels of mobility creates health problems for smaller sub-groups within society.

2.1.2.4 Specific ecological developments

Every instance of the development of more infrastructure for mobility has led to the further 'fragmentation' of nature (which can only partially be compensated for by making so-called 'eco-ducts': that is, bridges over or under a road intended for animals only) and to the life of animals and people being more and more disturbed by the increasing noise levels. Transport infrastructure is fragmenting natural habitats, which is extremely difficult to reverse (EEA 2004). Also, knowledge about the health effects that transport has on people living near busy roads is a topic receiving increasing policy attention, leading to, for instance, lower speed limits when atmospheric conditions are worse.

Nowadays in Europe any significant new infrastructural project is subject to an environmental impact assessment (EIA) and wide stakeholder consultation. EIA began to appear in European Regulation around 1986. Although the command-and-control approach is often still necessary, its limitations are increasingly apparent. Command-and-control strategies are ill equipped to deal with highly complex issues and do not respond well to public environmental concerns (Watson 2003).

Another development is that the new European air-quality standard is difficult to realise in densely populated areas and near busy roads. This already has led to drastic speed-reduction measures as the only possible short-term solution to keep pollution below the limit.

Climate issues have risen high on the political agenda in many countries and internationally. Moreover, public concern and debate about climate issues is extensive in many countries. A significant increase in attention to this issue has become apparent within the past couple of years, following a number of years receiving more moderate attention from the public. Whether this change is a permanent change or a more temporary phenomenon is still an open question. Also, the extent of media coverage of climate problems has widened.

2.1.3 Key systemic sustainability problems in the mobility domain

There are three clearly unsustainable ('triple C') issues in the mobility area:

- The ever-increasing levels of CO_2 emissions, which are tightly coupled to economic growth and that to date have been very hard to decouple, attributable to increased use of car and air transport and increased use of bigger cars

- The congestion problems with car mobility at peak hours in densely populated urban areas. This creates problems in all three dimensions of sustainability, causing environmental problems (more emissions per kilometre), social problems (loss of time to be spent on other private activities) and economic problems (loss of working hours for professionals spending time in traffic jams)

- The still high rate of casualties and injured people on the roads. On a world scale the number of yearly road traffic fatalities is about one million people (WBCSD 2004) whereas air traffic creates approximately

FIGURE 2.2 Trends in energy consumption, emissions of carbon dioxide (CO$_2$),
GDP, road fatalities and acidifying emissions

Source: EEA 2002

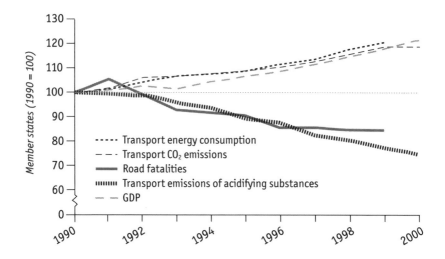

1,500 fatalities per year. This high death toll evidently has significant social affects on the families of the victims. Additional passive safety measures (such as the use of safety belts, heavier cars with less-deformable cages, airbags, etc.) have added costs to the purchase and use of cars and generally have also increased environmental emissions because of the greater weight to be produced and transported. In some countries, a measure such as the introduction of speed limits for safety reasons can reduce casualties and emissions per kilometre (although in Germany a speed limit on the autobahn does not make the traffic more safe, according to traffic experts)

Climate-affecting emissions evidently are not the only environmental issue connected to mobility. Local pollution, health, noise and visual pollution are also at issue. The so-called polluting emissions from road transport have been significantly decoupled from economic growth in the past 15 years as a result of the Euro and fuel composition standards.

A number of environmental impacts arising from the area of mobility have social impacts as well and are not equally distributed across social classes or across societies. Although noise pollution and visual impacts tend to affect all, they do tend to affect poorer parts of the population more than they do the richer parts.

2.2 The mobility system (regime) and windows of opportunity

2.2.1 Production–consumption chain and interlinked practices: the 'regime'

The main actors within the regime for mobility are summarised in simplified graphical form in Figure 2.3.

In fact, the real interactions and production chain are far more complex. Authorities interact with all players through investments, regulation, innovation support, promotion campaigns and so on. Quite often, responsibility for planning and maintenance of roads is split between national, regional and local authorities. Vehicle producers (e.g. of cars, aeroplanes, trains, buses) have many specialised suppliers that provide parts to them. In the car industry this has led to a significant amount of standardisation of components and technologies, yet vehicle producers have a need to develop and sell different products to different consumers because the survival economies of scale in the vehicle industry are

FIGURE 2.3 Regime actors related to physical artefacts in the mobility system

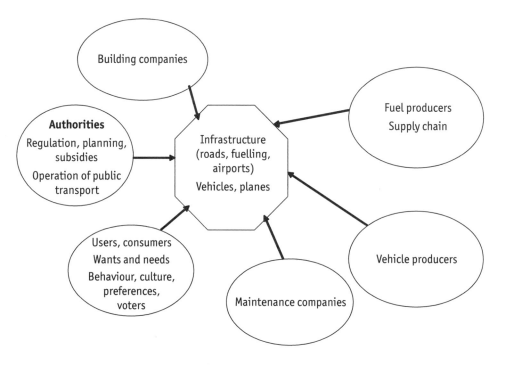

extremely important because of the high levels of investment. Economies of scale promoted standardisation of components. Standardisation tends to be a strong stabilising factor because any new solution has to start competing right from the start. Standardisation can also be a favourable condition for fast, wide-scale implementation of more sustainable technological solutions for components. The production chain for aeroplanes is different in the sense that there are only a few main players left in the market (Boeing, Airbus) and an aeroplane is much more complex than a car, typically containing many more parts (in the order of a million). For buses, there are many more producers than there are for aeroplanes.

The sociotechnical regime that allowed the transport system in Western society to grow over the past century can be characterised by a game with four main players:

- Authorities that are responsible for providing and maintaining public infrastructure for transport (although railway companies often started as private companies), including all associated regulation. Authorities or public bodies are usually also responsible for the operation of public transport. Recently, the concept of privatisation as a means to increase competition and improve service levels has been introduced in public transport. Private investments in public infrastructure are encouraged by public authorities (as, for instance, the *péage* in France) in recent years, most probably to reduce public investment levels

- Private producers of vehicles (of cars, trains, buses, etc.) that are free to develop and sell vehicles to customers such as individual consumers, companies and authorities

- Users (private and professional) that choose the best solution in terms of budget, time, quality and comfort for their own transport needs or wants

- Fuel producers and their outlets that provide any type of fuel

Evidently, private producers of vehicles have to fulfil the regulation imposed by authorities such as for safety or in relation to polluting emissions. The transport needs that people have is not a directly controllable issue for authorities as we are living in a free world and a free-market economy. Indirectly, authorities influence transport needs through policies controlling the spatial planning of living areas and economic activities, through labour policies or by influencing the price levels.

Mobility infrastructure has the character of a public good to be freely used by everybody as long as they pay for it through (in)direct taxes or tickets per usage. This has been the basic system paradigm of the free market for mobility.

Mobility solutions are often a combination of services provided to consumers by public institutions, with products or services provided by private enterprises offering transport systems, means of transport and a number of related services.

Public planning and infrastructure play a large role in the mobility area. When talking about the production and consumption system of this area, public planners, managers of transport systems and policy-makers inevitably take up a central position.

Road transport and cars have come to dominate the mobility systems in most countries, not only in the countryside and sparsely populated areas where individual transport has some clear advantages such as versatility in use and accessibility, but also in towns and urban areas where public transport and collective transport means are more 'natural'.

Authorities in the need area 'mobility' were and are heavily involved and have vested interests in the mobility system. They are the

- Providers and owners of road and public transport infrastructure

- Operators of public transport services (although privatisation is increasing)

- Regulators for safety, traffic rules, product standards and so on

- Collectors of the fuel, vehicle and road taxes and excises (for instance, in Belgium car and fuel taxes comprise 8% of the tax income of the state)

- Public procurers of mobility

To obtain a return on investment certain consumption levels are needed, but a strong reduction in road or public transport consumption level is not really desirable from the perspective of public finance, unless other sources of tax can compensate for losses.

An internal inconsistency in the present regime is the contradiction in transport systems that often is embedded in the single individual: people love their cars and good roads when they drive the car and need to go from one place to another in a fast and comfortable way. However, the rest of the time, and when it comes to the cars of other people, they see car transport and the ever-growing network of roads as a serious societal problem.

In different parts of the transport sector there is currently considerable focus on the environmental aspects of transport and mobility. For example, cars and the car industry are receiving much attention with regard to the environment, low-consumption cars, green cars and so on. This follows more than a decade where the focus in many countries was in the opposite direction: on the production of still larger cars (with greater fuel consumption), four-wheel drive vehicles and off-road cars.

In many countries train operators and bus operators are to an increasing degree referring to the environmental advantages of trains and buses in commercials and other communications to the wider public. The Eurostar train from London to Brussels, for instance, claims to produce a carbon footprint ten times smaller than the same trip by airplane.

In some countries the institutions managing the transport and mobility sector (e.g. road agencies, regional planning institutions, etc.) have changed and they now to some extent integrate environmental issues and sustainability in their planning. In other countries, the focus is still primarily on improving the opportunities for more mobility and more traffic.

The concept of mobility management is established as an issue of public planning as well as an issue for company policy.

2.2.2 Stability and windows of opportunity in the system

Consumers and systems usually cannot change rapidly because of stabilising trends or factors. Nonetheless, at certain moments in time windows of opportunity occur for actors to make decisions that can improve sustainability performance.

2.2.2.1 Stabilising trends or factors

Stabilising factors and trends are as follows:

- There have been two constant factors of importance for passenger transport demand. On average, people have tended to have a more or less fixed time budget for transport (the Brever law). Better and faster transport has led to the situation where, on average, people with better opportunities for faster transport will travel further, within these constant time limits. On the positive side, when congestion becomes too time-consuming this Brever law can lead also to changes in choices for work or living location

- People spend a more or less fixed share of their income on transport. Price elasticity is different in the short term compared with the long term. In the short term consumers are 'locked in' because of their own situation and cannot significantly reduce travelling when prices go up (that is, there is high price inelasticity in the short term). In the long term (over several years) people can adapt their needs and/or wants to higher price levels (changing the location of where they work or live, choosing to buy a car with lower levels of fuel consumption, reducing their leisure activities and so on)

- Globalisation has reached its limits in the sense that transport distances within the production chain of products cannot grow much more; it is only the number of different suppliers of subcomponents or processes that might still grow as a result of further specialisation

- A stabilising factor is the very high inertia with regard to system components as a result of economic depreciation. Typical lifetimes are:
  - Infrastructure: tens to hundreds of years
  - Aeroplanes: 20–30 years
  - Cars: 10–15 years

- Stabilising factors also come from the economy of scale demands in the production chain: past high investments in technology create path dependence. Totally new and young technology needs an incubator (protected niche market) to get ready for full market competition. The long-term perspective should be high enough to allow for losses in the beginning (before a return on investment)

- A stabilising factor for congestion is, strangely enough, congestion itself. Only when congestion becomes 'painful' will commuters start searching for alternative routes and modes of transport or reconsider their work and home locations

2.2.2.2 Destabilising factors for the mobility regime
Destabilising factors for the mobility regime arise from:

- Geopolitical tensions and the associated insecurity of oil supply

- The increasing general concern, through increased media attention, about climate change

- Awareness and action from those sub-groups in society that suffer the greatest health effects as a consequence of air pollution and nuisance, creating at least a local force against unlimited growth

- The rise of external costs

- Zero-emission vehicle regulation in California, creating a shock to the car manufacturing industry, although the requirements have been postponed and watered down during the years (Hekkert and van den Hoed 2006)

2.2.2.3 Windows of opportunity for consumers and producers

The consumption side

Within the mobility area the main windows of opportunity occur at the so-called big decisions or changes in life: getting or changing a job, buying a house, getting married, having children, buying a car, etc. It is at these moments that big decisions are taken that determine to a large extent the behaviour and consumption patterns for many years to come by fixing the distance between work and home, by choosing the accessibility to public transport, by fixing the emissions of a vehicle, etc. After these moments of change, habits are created, as are social, professional or economic lock-ins that make more sustainable consumption patterns hard to achieve.

The production side

Every new investment project in infrastructure and every new technology or product platform for vehicles provides opportunities for more sustainable patterns of consumption. Evidently, basic research towards new more sustainable options need to experience success early on in order for developers to be able to take the option on board and develop it further during the project. Authorities should reward sustainable innovation based on the societal benefits the outcomes of the innovation might generate.

2.2.3 Typical strategies

In general, there are three main strategies for improving the sustainability of mobility. These strategies often have synergetic objectives or effects regarding the three main unsustainable issues relating to mobility (climate change, congestion and casualties):

- Reduce needs and wants
- Promote a shift to more sustainable (collective) modes of mobility
- Promote the sustainability performance of all modes of mobility

2.2.3.1 Reduction of needs and wants

This is the most conceptual approach, addressing the societal values, paradigms and organisation of almost all societal systems (labour regimes, leisure regimes). In fact, all actors in society have a role to play in this strategy. It requires a fundamental rethinking of the need or want to displace ourselves. Practical examples for reducing our needs or wants can be found in tax policy for house movers, planning policy that avoids urban sprawl, the use of the benefits of modern ICT technologies in working practices (such as teleworking), supporting job moves closer to home, internalising external costs leading to lower demand, and so on. In general, the strategy to achieve 'need reduction' requires solutions to many lock-in situations (economical, professional, social) and touches many other non-mobility policy areas. The focus of (public) investments should be on providing citizens with access to services within shorter distances or electronically and, as a consequence, discourage the need or urge to travel (EEB/ETUC 2003).

2.2.3.2 Promotion of a shift to more sustainable (collective) modes of mobility

This strategy comprises, for example, investment in a high-speed rail networks (for shorter distances, to replace air transport), car sharing (with limited success so far), company mobility plans to improve biking infrastructure in urban areas, solving the private–public transport gap by building park-and-ride locations, promoting train taxis, introducing easy bike-hire systems (as in Paris 2007) and so on.

Such change can be stimulated by price mechanisms or voluntary initiatives. Evidently, if authorities call for voluntary efforts from other actors within society they should provide a good example as well by Green Public Procurement (GPP), mobility policy for state employees (for example, state employees in The Netherlands are no longer allowed to take aeroplanes to destinations less than 300 km away) and so on.

Whenever the strategy is based on reducing car transport and shifts to more collective public transport modes, positive effects are expected for the three unsustainable issues (reduction of CO_2 emissions, congestion and casualties).

2.2.3.3 Promotion of the sustainability performance of each mode of mobility

This strategy includes technological improvements in internal combustion engines, alternative technologies based on other engine types, reducing losses of any nature and so on. Here there is a clear task for industry, research and innovation (practical examples are the development of the Smart® car and the upcoming very efficient LOREMO® sports car in Germany, traffic management by Intelligent Transport Systems, electrification of rail transport and more efficient engines for aeroplanes). Some, but definitely not all, examples within this strategy can also reduce congestion. Technological improvements such as further CO_2 reduction for cars are feasible (Nieuwenhuis 2007) but will not be enough to achieve overall sustainability (Åkerman and Höjer 2006).

There are attempts to include what the environmental economists call 'the external costs' (the cost of environmental impacts that are not covered directly by producers and consumers) in the economic analysis and planning in the mobility area. At present, most of these costs are not included in the prices of transport, other mobility services or in the costs of infrastructure and planning activities. The value of external costs is estimated to be 7.3% of GDP for the EU-17 in 2004, a figure that does not include congestion costs (OECD 2006).

Much can be gained through a 'green' formation of prices and markets in the mobility area. Many have also pointed to the fact, however, that the achievement of a completely fair price formation that includes everything is not possible because of the complexity of the system; and therefore market prices cannot form the only means of handling the environmental aspects of mobility. The instrument of internalising external costs can play a role in all three typical strategies, creating positive rebound effects.

The cases that are described in the following chapters have been selected on the basis of several arguments; in order to derive a variety of lessons they will show:

FIGURE 2.4 The relation between the case studies in this book to the strategies to improve the mobility domain and to reduce the three main problems within this domain: carbon dioxide (CO_2) emissions, congestion and casualties

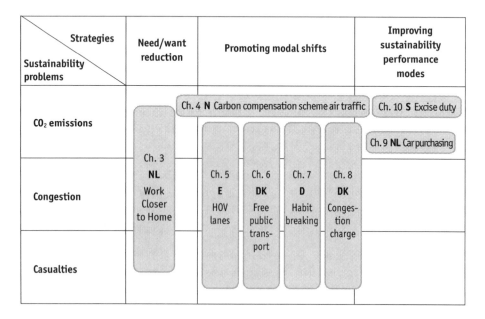

- A clear link to or influence from user and/or consumer behaviour

- A wide variety of approaches (creating changes across the system components of infrastructure, vehicles and behaviour)

- Different mobility modes

- A variety of examples across Europe

In Figure 2.4 one can see how the cases belong to the typical strategies and how they relate to the three main sustainability problems within the mobility domain.

References

Åkerman, J., and M. Höjer (2006) 'How Much Transport Can the Climate Stand? Sweden on a Sustainable Path in 2050', *Energy Policy* 34: 1,944-57.

Beckx, C., T. Arentze , L. Int Panis, D. Janssens, J. Vankerkom and G. Wets (2009) 'An Integrated Activity-Based Modelling Framework to Assess Vehicle Emissions: Approach and Application', *Environment and Planning B: Planning and Design* in press.

EEA (European Environment Agency) (2002) *Paving the Way for EU Enlargement: TERM 2002 Summary* (Copenhagen: EEA).

—— (2004) *Ten Key Transport and Environment Issues for Policy-makers* (Number 3; Copenhagen: EEA).

—— (2005) *Household Consumption and the Environment* (Number 11; Copenhagen: EEA).

—— (2006a) *Transport and Environment: Facing a Dilemma* (Number 3; Copenhagen: EEA).

—— (2006b) *Urban Sprawl in Europe, The Ignored Challenge* (Number 10; Copenhagen, Denmark: EEA).

—— (2007) *Transport and Environment: On the Way to a New Common Transport Policy: TERM 2006* (Number 1; Copenhagen: EEA).

—— (2009) *Transport at a Crossroads. TERM 2008: Indicators Tracking Transport and Environment in the European Union* (Number 3; Copenhagen: EEA).

EEB/ETUC (European Environmental Bureau/European Trade Union Confederation) (2003) 'Manifesto for Sustainable Investment: Investing for a Sustainable Future', November 2003; etuc.org/a/1472, accessed 25 February 2009.

EU (1999) '2165th Council meeting ENVIRONMENT Brussels, 11 March 1999' (press release on ACEA covenant); europa.eu/rapid/pressReleasesAction.do?reference=PRES/99/71&format=HTML&aged=1&language=EN&guiLanguage=en, accessed 14 July 2009.

—— (2001) *White Paper: European Transport Policy for 2010: Time to Decide* (Luxembourg: Office for Official Publications of the European Communities).

—— (2006) *Keep Europe Moving: Mid-term Review of the European Commission's 2001 Transport White Paper* (Brussels: Directorate General for Energy and Transport, European Commission).

—— (2008) Directive 2008/101/EC; eur-lex.europa.eu/LexUriServ/LexUriServ.do?uri=CELEX:32008L0101:EN:NOT, accessed 14 July 2009.

Hekkert, M., and R. van den Hoed (2006) 'Competing Technologies and the Struggle towards a New Dominant Design: The Emergence of the Hybrid Vehicle at the Expense of the Fuel-cell Vehicle?', in P. Nieuwenhuis, P. Vergragt and P. Wells (eds.), *The Business of Sustainable Mobility: From Vision to Reality* (Sheffield, UK: Greenleaf Publishing): 45-60.

Holden, E. (2007) *Achieving Sustainable Mobility: Everyday and Leisure-Time Travel in the EU* (Sogndal, Norway: Western Norway Research Institute).

Hoogma, R., R. Kemp, J. Schot and B. Truffer (2002) *Experimenting for Sustainable Transport: The Approach of Strategic Niche Management* (London: E & FN Spon).

Hupkes, G. (1982) 'The Law of Constant Travel Time and Trip Rate', *Futures* (February 1982): 38-46.

Jalas, M. (2002) 'A Time Use Perspective on the Materials Intensity of Consumption', *Ecological Economics* 41.1: 109-23.

Jensen, M. (1999) 'Passion and Heart in Transport: A Sociological Analysis on Transport Behaviour', *Transport Policy* 6: 19-33.

Nieuwenhuis, P. (2007) 'Car CO_2 Reduction Feasibility Assessment: Is 130 g/km Possible?' (Centre for Business Relationships, Accountability, Sustainability and Society; available at www.lowcvp.org.uk/assets/reports/CO2report_Cardiff_Univ_07.pdf, accessed 17 March 2009).

——, P. Vergragt and P. Wells (eds.) (2006) *The Business of Sustainable Mobility: From Vision to Reality* (Sheffield, UK: Greenleaf Publishing).

OECD (Organisation for Economic Cooperation and Development) (2006) *Decoupling the Environmental Impacts of Transport from Economic Growth* (Paris: OECD).

Rispens, S.I. (2003) 'De gevleugelde mens', *Intermediair* (The Netherlands) 48.

UK Department of Transport (2006) 'UK National Travel Survey 2006'; www.statistics.gov.uk/cci/nugget.asp?id=441, accessed 14 July 2009.

UNEP (United Nations Environment Programme)/EEA (European Environment Agency) (2007) *Sustainable Consumption and Production in South East Europe and Eastern Europe, Caucasus and Central Asia* (Copenhagen: UNEP/EEA).

Watson, M. (2003) 'Environmental Impact Assessment and European Community Law', paper presented at the 14th International Conference, 'Danube: River of Cooperation', Beograd, 13–15 November 2003.

WBCSD (World Business Council for Sustainable Development) (2004) 'Mobility 2030: Meeting the Challenges to Sustainability'; www.wbcsd.org/web/publications/mobility/mobility-full.pdf, accessed 14 July 2009.

3
Work Closer to Home
A web-based service to reduce home–work travel

S.J.F.M. Maase and J.W.A. Dekker

VU Amsterdam in cooperation with Adapt BV, The Netherlands

The Netherlands faces the rising problem of congestion on the main Dutch highways. The daily flow of commuters of 2.8 million out of a population of around 16 million is getting out of control, especially in the most populated areas such as the Randstad (Amsterdam, Utrecht, The Hague and Rotterdam). In these areas among 350,000–550,000 people get stuck in traffic jams daily while travelling to and from work by car. The economic damage is estimated to be in billions of euros. The negative effects on the environment and on the public's health are becoming more and more visible. In this chapter, we describe a private bottom-up initiative representing a new solution to the problem of reduced mobility caused by traffic jams.

A website (www.werkdichterbijhuis.nl, accessed 18 March 2009) stimulates people to exchange their job with someone having a similar job, but closer to their home. The primary goal is to reduce the daily flow of commuters, thus reducing the number and length of traffic jams. The initiators of this case, living in the Randstad, were confronted daily with traffic jams, being commuters themselves. The idea for the web-based service for commuters was born while being stuck in a traffic jam during the autumn of 2005. Discussing the idea with possible partners and consumers convinced the initiators to start the initiative. A website was developed and tested during 2006. To promote and strengthen the service, cooperation was sought with national government, job recruiters and interest groups. The site was launched in September 2006.

For the first year the initiators' aim was to establish public awareness of the web-based service for job exchange to more than 50% among the total number of commuters in The Netherlands. This case is an example of system innovation: it is about building a network of organisations working together to achieve a goal.

3.1 Case description

3.1.1 Overview

3.1.1.1 Problem definition

Traffic jams account for a number of problems for various stakeholders in society. The Netherlands houses Europe's largest port, in Rotterdam. Owing to lost hours caused by traffic jams, the transport sector loses €1.2 billion a year based on calculations made in 2002 (TLN 2002). The government tries to reduce the problem of congestion by building extra roads or temporary lanes used during rush hours, and plans to introduce payments per kilometre travelled are on the verge of being introduced. Mobility and transport interest groups focus on so-called quality networks, seeking to solve the problem at the most affected locations or trying to separate in time or space the transport of goods and people. These measures try to minimise the congestion but do not entail solutions that take into consideration the source of the problem: car drivers. Every day in The Netherlands 2.8 million people travel from home to work and then from work to home by car. Every day in the western part of The Netherlands, the Randstad, about 350,000–550,000 people get stuck in traffic jams while travelling to or from their place of work by car. In addition to the financial costs to society arising from congestion, there is a significant social effect on the individual. The extra time spent on travelling can take up a significant amount of an individual's time. Thirty minutes of traffic jam to and from work each day adds up to five hours a week that could be spent on family and social activities, rest, leisure and the like.

Indirect costs to employers include lost time from employees being late to work and increased absence because of illness. Employees facing traffic jams search daily for alternatives closer to home. These opportunities nevertheless are limited because of the decreasing number of vacancies and perceived difficulties in finding interesting alternatives. The creation of more vacancies is not easy and is highly dependent on the economic situation. The question now arises: how do we create new vacancies that fulfil the needs of the employee to have an interesting job close to home to reduce travel time significantly and preferably not to use a car?

3.1.1.2 Project goals

The primary goal of developing and implementing the project 'www. werkdichterbijhuis.nl', a web-based service called 'Work Closer to Home', is to significantly lower the amount of traffic during rush hours. The solution focuses on stimulating commuters to switch or change jobs, thus reducing travel time and distance. The lower level of traffic is attained by offering a valuable and realistic alternative in terms of employment closer to home. At the starting point of the project there was no tool or service for individuals to easily find a vacancy offering a comparable job to the current one but much closer to home.

The aim of the website is to become the largest platform for various stakeholders in the value chain of job trading to exchange information aimed at finding and providing a job closer to home. The primary focus is to connect two people (employees) who want to switch or change jobs in order to reduce their travel distance—and commute time. Other stakeholders involved are: employers, recruiters, job vacancy sites, local and national government, and transport or mobility interest groups.

A study in The Netherlands shows that with a 10% reduction of cars on the roads during rush hour, a 40% decrease in traffic jams can be expected (see TLN 2002). A survey organised by the initiator of this project, involving interviewing the target group, found that about 50% of the daily car drivers considered changing job or would like to consider changing jobs, if a good alternative is easily accessible. The project will be considered to be successful when 10% of the daily road users (280,000 car users) has switched or changed jobs, thus reducing travel time and distance and preferably not making use of roads while travelling from home to work and vice versa.

To be able to reach this goal the first target is to create public awareness of the existence of the project. Within the first 6–12 months after the launch of the website half of the 2,800,000 daily road users knew about the project. Within 12 months of the launch about 90% of the target group had heard about the initiative and the website. Within one year of the website launch about 30,000–70,000 participants were active at the website and available for a job switch.

The subscription of people on the website creates a large pool of jobs, a pool as large as the number of subscriptions. This creates greater flexibility as well as greater liquidity in the job market as a whole and makes the project interesting for job recruiters and vacancy sites to participate.

3.1.1.3 Solution description

The website www.werkdichterbijhuis.nl plays a central role in this case. For this reason we describe here the working of the site in more detail. The website provides the platform for people to search for and connect to other people who are also interested in switching jobs with fellow participants on the website or in changing jobs, by responding to the job offers. In order to lower the threshold for people to subscribe and to provide some information about their current job, subscription is free. Once a person has subscribed he or she can log on to a personalised page where he or she sees tailor-made matches: possible job switches with other participants and available job vacancies from partner vacancy sites in the area where the participant lives.

A participant (participant A) can signal another participant in the database with whom he or she would like to get in touch (participant B). Participant B now gets an automatically generated message telling him or her someone would like to get in touch to discuss a possible job switch. The job description is included anonymously. As soon as participant B also signals interest, the system will recognise this mutual agreement and releases the private and confidential information by email to the two participants. The individuals are now able to discuss privately their jobs and a possible switch. In due time, each individual pays to Adapt BV, which administers the system (see Section 3.1.3.1), a small amount of money for obtaining the detailed information about the job and job owner.

Job recruiters and vacancy sites are connected to the website in order to provide a larger pool of jobs for participants. When entering his or her private site the participant immediately sees an up-to-date list of vacancies available in the region where he or she lives.

3.1.2 Case context

The consumer or car user plays a dominant role in the success of this project. He or she has to be motivated to change or switch jobs in order to gain the benefits of reduced travel time and distance. The direct benefits of reduced travel time mentioned by car users are: time to take care of and spend with one's family, time to do sports, time to sleep and so on (Schreuder 2007). All these benefits would improve the individual's perceived quality of life and include indirect economic benefits such as a reduction in money spent on child care and expected positive health effects. Nevertheless, one of the paradigmatic views that applies to this case is that people search for solutions that have to be executed by parties other than themselves. Government and the transport sector should take action to reduce the amount of traffic jams by building more roads and by promoting travelling at hours outside the rush hour. A sense of consumer lock-in is present: finding another job as interesting and as good as the current one but closer to home is often perceived to be complex and difficult, and moving in order to live closer to work is not desirable or possible because of family circumstances, preferred area to live and so on. Nevertheless, 62% of the respondents to Adapt BV's survey are interested in an internet tool that makes job switching available and relatively easy.

Government works on both technical and motivational solutions to solve the congestion problem. The creation of more roads, rush-hour lanes and systems to manage traffic do contribute to reduced traffic pressure on Dutch roads, but still the number and length of traffic jams increases. Trying to change the car user's behaviour is difficult and based mainly on financial incentives such as the planned introduction of a pay-as-you-drive tax system.

3.1.3 Actors and their roles and perspectives

3.1.3.1 Primary actors

Adapt BV
Adapt BV is a small enterprise that initiated and developed the Work Closer to Home project. Two people work full-time on the project, the development and improvement of the website, the promotion of the website and the creation of partnerships with the other actors mentioned below in this paragraph. A group of testers is involved to give feedback on the functionalities and working of the website. Technical and design support is hired. The initiators Mrs A. Los and Mr J.W.A. Dekker are highly motivated to make the enterprise a success. Their motivation is based on a combination of the primary goal to significantly lower the amount of traffic during the rush hour with the commercial potential of their idea.

Employees and commuters
The target group the project focuses on is the 2.8 million road users in The Netherlands who daily use their car to drive from home to work and vice versa. This group can be divided into three sub-groups:[1]

- Male and female, between 25 and 35 years old: 52% of the total number of daily road users

- Male and female, between 36 and 45 years old: 32% of the total number of daily road users

- The remaining group of people younger than 25 and older than 45 years old: 16% of the total number of daily road users

1 The following figures are based on a survey made by Adapt BV of 505 commuters, interviewed at fuel stations all over The Netherlands during the rush hour in September 2006.

The project focuses both on the people in the target group who perceive their travel distance and time as too long (45% of the target group) and on the people who say that travel time is acceptable (55% of the target group). The reason for not distinguishing between these two groups is the fact that, from Adapt BV's survey, irrespective of the perceived travel time, both groups state they are potential users of the website (62% of the target group expressed an interest in the web-based service). This shows that the complete target group to a greater or lesser extent is open to switching or changing jobs in order to decrease travel time.

Job recruiters and vacancy sites

Participation of job recruiters and (existing) vacancy sites is of vital importance for the successful introduction of the web-based service. At the start of the project the number of employees subscribing to the website will be low, so the chance to find a job-switch match is equally low. Linking existing vacancy sites to the Work Closer to Home site, including a selection tool for employees to select existing vacancies close to home, increases the chance of an employee finding such a job. In the future, job recruiters might also play a role in facilitating a job switch once a match is made by two employees. Vacancy sites and job recruiters are very motivated to join the project. Next to publicity for their own sites and services, the Work Closer to Home site, once filled with subscribed members, provides a pool of people on the job market who otherwise would have been invisible and out of the reach of job recruiters.

3.1.3.2 Secondary actors

Government

Governmental support will enhance the successful implementation of this project and the creation of broader social support. At the moment government examines various options to change people's behaviour with regard to car use. The Work Closer to Home project creates a tool for people to change their behaviour willingly. Co-development of this project together with governmental measures currently under construction may lead more easily to solutions to congestion problems. Governmental measures currently under construction include the introduction of a pay-as-you-drive tax system, creating an incentive for job switching.

Multinationals and employers

Multinationals based in The Netherlands are considered to be interesting partners for the promotion and use of the web-based service of Work Closer to Home. The benefits for a multinational joining the Work Closer to Home project can be of two different kinds, depending on how the company wants to link to the initiative. First, a multinational can enhance its corporate social and environmental responsibility by stimulating employees to switch jobs internally in order to reduce travel time and distance. This is expected to lead, for example, to a reduction in absence due to illness as well as in CO_2 emissions by employees travelling long distances. Second, a multinational may strengthen its corporate image by promoting the Work Closer to Home initiative together with its products. Multinationals considered to be interested in linking to the initiative are oil companies, banks and multinationals in the consumer goods industry. Reasons for multinationals to have reservations about the project are the risks involved in joining a new and innovative initiative. A corporate image can be seriously damaged if a project does not prove to be successful. In some cases companies claim their employees already live close to their work, but exact figures are not available. Introducing a new project such as this and enrolling the support and participation of multinationals appears to be more complex and time-consuming than originally expected by the initiators of the project.

Interest groups
Cooperation with interest groups is sought by the initiators to increase public awareness and name recognition of the Work Closer to Home website and service. In many cases members of interest groups are part of the target group. Private individuals as well as the transport sector are interested in cooperating and inform others in their group about the initiative.

3.1.4 Potential sustainability performance

The project provides a new solution to the problem of congestion in The Netherlands. The primary aim of the project is to reduce the length and number of traffic jams. In order to estimate the potential change in sustainability performance from this project has been compared with two other basic approaches to reducing congestion: the 'pay-as-you-drive' approach and the 'technology-and-construction' approach. The pay-as-you-drive approach at this moment is being developed and discussed by the Dutch government but has not yet been introduced. The technology-and-construction approach entails all measures to reduce existing traffic pressure: the construction of extra roads, traffic management systems and so on. A qualitative description of expected improvements is given below, supported by the scores in Table 3.1 (Section 3.1.5).

The evaluation is based on the assumption that the primary and ambitious target of the project is met: to reduce the number of daily commuters by 10%, which means 280,000 people will have to switch jobs. This target is expected to decrease the number and length of traffic jams by 40% (see TLN 2002).

3.1.4.1 Environmental improvement

Environmental improvement deals with the reduction of emissions, material efficiency and space for nature. Exact calculations have not been made so far. Promising estimates have been constructed from various statistics and numbers, but are not elaborated in depth here.

- CO_2 and NO_x emissions will decrease depending on the reduction of car traffic and the effects of the more combustion-efficient transportation of goods

- Material efficiency is related to the reduced need to build extra roads or technology for traffic management. The sources to take into consideration for calculating material reduction effects are broad and impossible to calculate at short notice. Estimates could be made by mobility experts

- Space for nature. The reduced need to build extra roads creates space for nature and improves the natural environment of The Netherlands

3.1.4.2 Social improvements

Social improvements include social effects for both employer and employee. Quality of life will improve when travel time and distance to work is reduced. Nevertheless, before taking action the employee or potential job switcher has to evaluate the benefits of less travel time and shorter distance compared with the current job and its benefits. Cultural and behavioural changes are of vital importance for this project to succeed.

The employer having employees who are travelling less in terms of time and distance will experience less absence due to illness. Less travel time might also have an effect on employee stress.

3.1.4.3 Economic improvement

The concept of Work Closer to Home provides a commercially interesting solution. Profit will be generated from the exchange of contact details of potential job switchers and having these participants pay a fee for each exchange of contact details using www.werkdichterbijhuis.nl. For employers and vacancy sites the concept provides access to a pool of potential employees who would not be visible without this website, thus enhancing flexibility in the job market.

Economic sustainability might decrease if the project proves to be successful or if congestion is otherwise reduced. Once the congestion problem is solved, the motivation to switch jobs to avoid congestion disappears. A wave-like movement over time in congestion problems might become visible in the future.

3.1.5 Case history and development

The Work Closer to Home project started in 2005. Table 3.1 describes the various activities and results of the past four years. During this time the project has developed rapidly. A division in phases is defined to clarify the development of the project. As is the case of most projects in which the establishment of a network of cooperating partners is vital to the successful development of the idea, phases do not take place successively but in a spiral-like manner, repeating steps and building on experience gained throughout the process.

3.1.5.1 The 'kick-off'

The project began with the selection and establishment of an organisational structure to house the development and implementation of the new service.

3.1.5.2 Research and development of the web-based service

The research and development phase focused on the development of the web-based service in line with the expectations and interests of the intended users of the service. A survey was conducted by Adapt BV in September 2006 among 505 commuters. This survey revealed that 45% of the commuters surveyed perceived their travel time from home to work as being too long; 55% judged travel time to be acceptable. Nevertheless, of this larger group 62% of the respondents considered themselves to be potential users of the web-based service as proposed by Adapt BV. Connecting these figures to the contextual consumer lock-in as described in Section 3.1.2, the challenge for the development of the web-based service is to provide a high-quality service that is both easy to use and effective.

The development of the web-based service included close cooperation with potential users to obtain feedback on the working and visual appearance of the website. Multiple design loops were necessary to create the website, and improvements are continuously being made based on user feedback.

3.1.5.3 Establishment of partnerships

The establishment of partnerships was essential for the development of the Work Closer to Home concept. The primary focus in searching for partners was on partners in the promotion of the service and partners to provide financial support for the initiative. As in many bottom-up cases for sustainable development, the search for and finding of partners is a trial-and-error, repetitive activity consuming a lot of time and energy. The first challenge for the initiators was to explain the concept clearly to the potential partner, awakening his or her interest. As the concept is completely new, scepticism was met when presenting the concept. The second challenge was to determine the partner's specific reason for

TABLE 3.1 Development timetable

Time	Activity	Results
September 2005	Being stuck in a traffic jam	Idea for web-based service was born
October 2005	Organisational structure established Search for partners started	Start Adapt BV
October 2005 to April 2006	Elaboration of idea Writing of requests for funding	
April 2006 to September 2006	Design and construction of website Testing of website with users Adjusting of website Search for partners	www.werkdichterbijhuis.nl Cooperating partners: ● Vacancy site ● Interest group
October 2006 to December 2006	Launch of website Extension of the number of cooperating partners	
January 2007 to April 2007	Extension of the number of cooperating partners to promote the website	Media attention creates increasing traffic at the site. All large Dutch vacancy sites are linked to the website
May 2007–June 2008	Work Closer to Home initiators seek to get connected to business sector/multinationals for cooperation	It appears very difficult to motivate CEOs of multinationals to collaborate with (as it was at that time) a small partner like Work Closer to Home
June–July 2008	Various discussions with the Taskforce Mobility Management (TFMM) of the Dutch Ministry of Transport, Public Works and Water Management	Partnership between TFMM and a number of organisations including Work Closer to Home
March–April 2009	Quantitative research among 500 commuters in the Haaglanden region by order of TFMM	Knowledge and insight about how commuters experience and deal with mobility issues.
May–June 2009	TFMM in close cooperation with the external partners writes the project proposal 'Living and Working'	Project proposal
July–September 2009	Preparation of pilot project by all partners involved	Pilot project in the Haaglanden region will begin in autumn 2009

why he or she would or would not participate in the initiative. In this process new ideas were often adopted on how the partner could join, adapting the primary intention of the initiators on how to collaborate with the specific partner.

Partnerships with vacancy sites and job recruiters were developed relatively quickly. The potential benefits of participating in the initiative for these actors are clear and the risks of participation low. The same went for the interest groups who more or less provide the role of promoting the initiative in society. The process of enrolling government and multinationals was more complex, for various reasons: government at various levels is interested in the initiative, but government's internal focus for solving the congestion problem was on technological and financial measures. In 2008 various organisations, both commercial and public, approached the Ministry of Transport, Public Works and Water Management independently. The Taskforce Mobility Management of the ministry brought these parties together. They collaborated to create a project proposal, which combines living and working as an integrated approach to solving congestion problems per region. For multinationals the risk of damaging their corporate image in the case of failure is high; in addition to this, they spend a lot of money on recruiting employees. At first sight, the promotion of job switching seems to work against such investment and to add to the costs of employment.

3.1.5.4 Implementation: launch and promotion of the website

For a successful and convincing website launch it is important to create a high level of participation in a very short time (the level of participation equals the number of subscribed users, providing information about their job for job-switching purposes). This requires an intense and focused promotion campaign. Radio commercials during rush hours and daily magazine advertisements are considered to be effective ways to achieve attention. Free publicity such as news items on television help to create public awareness and name recognition. Various actors such as vacancy sites, job recruiters and interest groups are actively involved in the promotion of the website. To reduce the risk of a low participation level vacancy sites are also involved in promoting and linking their vacancies on the website, thus creating extra value for the initial users.

3.1.5.5 Follow-up

As soon as the greater part of the target group is familiar with the web-based service for switching jobs, promotion activities will have to be focused on stimulating the use of the service over time. Another group that has to get actively involved in promoting and supporting this service consists of the employers. A more flexible attitude towards the switching of jobs and mentality change will have to be developed and anchored in Dutch companies if the project is to work. Activities to be taken into consideration are, for example, ways to inform human resource management departments and employee interest organisations about the project and how to deal with individuals proposing a job switch. The project proposal 'Living and Working in . . .' includes close cooperation with human resource departments of companies in a region.

3.2 Results

3.2.1 Main results

The website www.werkdichterbijhuis.nl was launched in October 2006. Results are described based on measurements taken half a year after the website launch (end of April 2007 and June 2009).

3.2.1.1 Achievements and unexpected results

Without having the financial means to invest heavily in targeted public relations, the initiators were nevertheless able to attract a lot of free publicity. News items on television and articles in a number of national and renowned newspapers and magazines resulted in thousands of people visiting the website in the first month after launch. About 10% of the visitors became active participant or 'job switchers' with his or her personal profile on the website. Towards the end of 2008 the website counted 20,000 participants. Thanks to collaboration with vacancy sites the website has become a platform and meeting place for job searchers, job switchers and job providers. Since January 2007 recruiters and human resource managers in workplaces have been using the site to place vacancies. They are referred to the site providers to submit their vacancy.

The website was developed with a minimum of (financial) resources. The website works well but needs further improvement, especially with regard to back-office technology to be able to provide a high-quality service in future.

In 2008 the Ministry of Transport, Public Works and Water Management was contacted by various Dutch organisations with regard to addressing solutions for congestion problems in The Netherlands. The Ministries Taskforce Mobility Management (TFMM) arranged a meeting with all initiators, including Adapt BV and the Work Closer to Home initiative. The purpose of the meeting was to discuss the possibility of creating one strong collaborative proposal. This proposal resulted in a survey among commuters and companies in one of the most congested regions in The Netherlands. Perceptions and effects of the congestion problem on both personal life and company performance were investigated. The

TABLE 3.2 Overview of project targets and results

Target for nine months after website launch	Results April 2007 | June 2009
Level of participation of daily road users by free subscription to the website: 30,000–70,000 people	Number of users: ◦ April 2007: 9,000 ◦ December 2008: 20,000
Number of actual job switches	Unknown owing to error in the back-office design and the supply of statistical information New web-service company takes over the design
To reduce the average travel distance of 47 km from home to work to less than 23 km	Each user receives 10–15 job matches derived from the complete database; 2–3% of the users receive a job match for switching
Established partnerships with primary and secondary actors	**Job recruiters and vacancy sites:** four of the largest vacancy sites in the Netherlands joined the initiative in linking their databases to the website **Government:** the Ministry of Transport, Public Works and Water Management is highly interested. Since the second half of 2008 cooperation has begun. Further research has been executed in close cooperation. A pilot project has been defined (June 2009) and will begin in autumn 2009 **Multinationals and employers:** contacts are made, but no partnerships established yet **Interest groups:** established partnerships with VNO-NCW, Vereniging Mobiliteitsmanagement (VM2), www.hier.nu and van A naar Beter

general outcome of this research was that, despite economic recession, both employers and employees face problems due to congestion and are willing to search for and contribute to solutions. From this survey a pilot project was set up called 'Living and Working in . . .'. This project will collect and connect information with regard to living/housing and the job market in a region. It also promotes living and working in the various regions involved, and facilitates the process of working closer to home—or living closer to work—for both employers and employees. The pilot project will start in autumn 2009 in the Haaglanden region in The Netherlands.

3.2.1.2 Setbacks

Fewer participants have subscribed to the website than projected at the beginning of the project. One of the reasons is a lack of financial resources to promote the website in order to attract the attention of the target group. The traffic generated at the website after free publicity items on television and in newspapers shows there is a lot of interest. About 10% of the traffic generated at the site results in subscription and the creation of a profile by the visitor.

Strong financial partners were needed for sustainable success of the 'Work Closer to Home' initiative. Many CEOs of multinationals and large national companies have been approached but without tangible results. According to the project initiators, internal processes in one of the potential partner's organisations led to a no-go decision. In general this small unknown initiative didn't attract sufficient large-company attention. The collaborative pilot project 'Living and Working in . . .' transformed the opportunities for Work Closer to Home. Work Closer to Home is fully integrated in the pilot project.

3.2.2 Change in sustainability performance

Owing to the fact that www.werkdichterbijhuis.nl is connected to the databases of the five largest Dutch job vacancy sites, each member of the website receives 10–13 job offers closer to home based on his or her personal profile. Only estimates can be made about how many people actually switch jobs and the effects on sustainability performance (see Section 3.1.4). Although the initiators put effort in obtaining feedback from their members, it proved to be very difficult to receive detailed information from a significant number of participants about the actual effect of the website on their job-changing behaviour. For this reason quantitative sustainability performance is not measurable so far.

3.2.3 Learning experiences

3.2.3.1 According to the initiator . . .

A stimulating factor in the development of this project was the inspiring contact with various parties involved and potential partners. Almost everyone we approached showed great confidence in the concept and expressed their admiration with regard to the idea. We were surprised to be able to set up partnerships with four vacancy sites which otherwise are competitors. On our site they can be found 'hand in hand'. The fact that each three-month report on the development of traffic jams over the past year showed an increase provided us with facts and figures to communicate the seriousness of the problem to potential partners. Communicating the potential reduction of CO_2 emissions and the subsequent effect with regard to the issue of climate change has also created many opportunities to enrol new partners. It is clear to us that current discussions in society contribute to public awareness and interest in our web-based service. The challenge now will be to motivate people to take action and actually to switch jobs using the platform we provide on the internet.

One blocking factor in the development of the project has been the issue of confidentiality when starting to share the idea with potential partners. We did not want to reveal the idea in full because we feared a big company would copy our idea and, with their greater financial power, could develop and introduce it faster. At this moment there is one website providing a similar service.

Another blocking factor was the lack of financial means. In the start-up phase it was frustrating that the positive attitude and comments we receive did not translate into financial support. Nevertheless, the pilot project in cooperation with the Taskforce Mobility Management of the Ministry of Transport, Public Works and Water Management, Moviq, WorkingLife, UWV (Uitvoering werknemersverzekeringen) provides Adapt BV with the opportunity to work on a solution for the congestion problem.

3.2.3.2 Three important lessons learned . . .

- It was difficult to find partners who want to co-finance the project. The regional focus of the 'Living and Working in . . .' project is a successful strategy to attract companies in a region

- In general, the process of building partnerships is long and time-consuming—something that the initiator was not aware of beforehand. Research on how partnerships and networks are established and practical tools or advice on how to enhance this process would be very welcome not only to the initiators of this project but also to all initiators of similar bottom-up projects

- To date, the initiators have focused mainly on building partnerships and finding funding. An important factor for the success of this project is to motivate commuters to switch jobs. Strategies for changing their current behaviour have not been developed up till now. The pilot project 'Living and Working in . . .' seeks to provide the information and services needed in order for people to change their behaviour with regard to home–work travel

3.3 Potential for diffusion and scaling up

This project faces the usual difficulties that come with attempts to change the current behaviour of a number of actors in the system. The successful implementation of this solution depends highly on to what extent various actors are willing to take responsibility for the problem of congestion in The Netherlands. The national government is the main actor to take measures to solve this problem. The initiators' attention has been focused on establishing partnerships with multiple sectors in society, thus attempting to scale up the project. The pilot project in cooperation with the Taskforce Mobility Management and a number of other partners, as mentioned before, will start in one region in The Netherlands in autumn 2009. The results will be evaluated and used for implementing the project in other regions. The project is not only about solving the congestion problem but also about empowering actors in society by providing a job-switch tool. Interest has been shown internationally to launch the website in other countries as well. This opportunity has not been developed further as yet.

3.4 Concluding remarks

The Work Closer to Home case is a bottom-up initiative that represents an innovative solution to the problem of congestion. Below the surface this case deals with the complex issue of behavioural change at various levels in society. Employees are encouraged to take their fate in their own hands and reduce the time and energy spent on travelling from home to work by switching jobs. Employers are challenged to be flexible and to be open to the job-switching phenomenon and to identify the benefits to them in times of reduced availability of good employees.

The initiators of the project are taking the challenge to communicate with all actors and have put tremendous effort into enrolling the participation of others at all levels in society. The time has come to recognise the potential of this product and to focus on solving the source of the traffic jam problems instead of fighting the symptoms. Without partnerships, especially without influential partners such as national government, this would still be a hard fight.

References

Schreuder, A. (2007) 'Er komt geen eind aan', *M* (monthly magazine of NRC Handelsblad, Rotterdam), March 2007: 17-28.

TLN (Transport en Logistiek Nederland) (2002) *Timmeren aan de Weg: Visie van TLN op een effectief en efficiënt infrastructuurbelei* (Zoetermeer, Netherlands: Transport en Logistiek Nederland).

4
Carbon compensation scheme for air mobility in Norway

Mads Borup

Technical University of Denmark, Department of Management Engineering

As part of a new climate policy, the Norwegian government has stated that climate compensation is to be made for all international air travel made by state employees. The strategy of this climate gas compensation scheme is that this public effort will be a clear example to others and will lead companies and organisations as well as other countries to change to similar practices. Thereby, radical change in the climate impact of air traffic is expected to result.

The climate gas compensation scheme is one element in a new general climate policy for Norway in which it is acknowledged that the climate problem is one of the most important issues to be dealt with in coming years and that climate-changing emissions from transport must be reduced. Norway shall both reduce its own emissions and contribute to reductions in other countries.

For organisations other than state organisations, the climate gas compensation scheme is voluntary. A number of airline companies and travel agencies have established the needed tools and routines for calculating climate emissions and the corresponding compensation required in connection with flights. Also, a number of non-governmental organisations (NGOs) and companies specialising in the issue offer this opportunity. There is increasing demand among private and professional consumers for more climate-friendly travel in general, and for climate gas compensation systems in particular.

4.1 Case description

4.1.1 Overview and background

Air traffic and mobility by air have developed significantly in recent decades. The amount of business and private travel by air has increased considerably and air traffic today accounts for a considerable share of transport-related emissions of carbon dioxide (CO_2) and other greenhouse gases (EEA 2009). Emissions are expected to rise further in the future. It is acknowledged by many actors that a change in this development is needed; however, currently, no efficient methods to achieve this have been established. Unlike, for example, fuel for road transport in many countries, fuel used by aeroplanes is currently an unregulated area with respect to climate-damaging emissions. On domestic flights in Norway, however, the airline companies pay a CO_2 tax.

As in many other countries, climate change and the need to limit such change have in recent years risen high on the policy agenda in Norway, including in the transport and mobility area, where air traffic is an important element. Norwegian air traffic has increased by around 150% since 1990. The largest increases have occurred in international travel, which has tripled and now constitutes 85% of person-kilometres travelled (Tajet 2006). Climate gas emissions have grown accordingly (Finstad *et al.* 2002), constituting 11% of the total climate gas emissions from Norwegians.

Increased efforts to reduce climate gas emissions as well as the climate gas compensation scheme were announced as central messages in the New Year speech by Prime Minister Jens Stoltenberg at the beginning of 2007 (Stoltenberg 2007). It is thus a high-profile issue and the subject has subsequently been discussed in the mass media.

The public administration sector accounts for more than 20,000 air journeys per year. The government expects to compensate for 60,000 tons of CO_2 per year (Hammer 2007) and to spend between 6 and 12 million Norwegian krona (NKR) (€0.7–1.4 million) on the scheme. In parallel to the Norwegian compensation scheme, other public administrations—for example, the UK government—have taken steps similar to the practice of buying carbon compensation in connection with all air travel made by public employees.

4.1.2 Actors and their roles

4.1.2.1 Primary actors

International policy and the dialogue between the Norwegian government and governmental leaders in the European Union and in other countries played an important role in the establishment of the climate gas compensation scheme.

The commitment to international climate obligations is a challenge that is becoming all the more difficult to meet with continuously increasing traffic. The need for action has become more and more urgent. Though Norway is not a member of the European Union, public policy and regulation in Norway are on many levels developed in coordination with EU efforts. In the second half of 2006, the European Commission proposed a new directive regarding emission and trading schemes (EC 2006). It will by 2011 put a limit on CO_2 emissions from air traffic. That the EU has taken steps to implement measures in order to reduce the impact of climate gas from air traffic in EU countries is an important incentive for Norway to do something similar.

Many airline companies recognise the problems associated with climate gas emissions and are currently establishing strategies and practices that can meet these challenges. The airline companies are experiencing a growing demand from businesses and other customers to handle climate impacts related to travel. They also face international and national policy and regulation on the issue. The introduction of the climate gas compensation scheme for public employees in Norway is well coordinated with reinforced efforts by some airline companies. The scheme supports new efforts on the part of airline companies to offer carbon compensation for air travel. The scheme was not introduced before it was possible in practice for airline companies to offer the opportunity for carbon compensation.

The semi-public Scandinavian Airline Systems, SAS, is one of the most used airline companies for international travel from and to Norway. In the beginning of 2007, SAS introduced the opportunity for CO_2 compensation to its customers. The impact from air travel can be calculated at the internet homepage of the airline company (www.sas.no). Also, airline companies such as Widerøe, Blue 1, British Airways, Spanair and SAS Braathens (domestic flights) offer the opportunity of carbon compensation (*Boarding.no* 2007a, 2007b).

For a company such as SAS the effort is part of its environmental strategy. SAS wants to be known by the public as one of the leading airline companies concerning the limitation of environmental impact from air travel. Sustainable development, including environmental sustainability, has in recent years been a part of the business model for SAS. To act as a socially and environmentally responsible and aware company is important. SAS promotes itself in ways that can connect it to sustainability and environmental protection, and the provision of information about the environmental impacts to consumers and others is prioritised. Among the few, selected, key parameters that passengers meet in the brief information sheets about SAS aircrafts has thus in recent years been the fuel consumption per person-kilometre.

The company actively promotes the inclusion of aviation into the European emission trading system. In 2006, SAS met with the EU in order to discuss efforts toward sustainable development and the limitation of climate gas emissions from the air travel sector. SAS also, for example, advertises on the internet homepages of environmental NGOs. The environmental dimension have become a parameter of competition in the air travel area. Many discount airline companies have not established carbon compensation opportunities.

4.1.2.2 Other actors

Some of the actors indirectly involved in the establishment of the new public climate gas compensation scheme in Norway are as important as those directly involved, not least the EU, as mentioned above; and a number of NGOs have played important roles.

NGOs have been actively involved in various ways. A number of organisations announced relatively early in the process that they will pay compensation for their travel and that they support the use of the compensation scheme. A number of environmental NGOs, humanitarian organisations and organisations dedicated to the sustainable development of society have contributed actively to policy discussions and media debate about climate gas emissions and the compensation scheme. Moreover, they have carried out analyses as background for such discussion. They argue for an ambitious climate policy and see the climate gas compensation scheme as one of the elements in this. The organisations are, among others, Norges Naturvernforbund (Friends of the Earth Norway), Kirkens Nødhjælp (Norwegian Church Aid) and Framtiden i våre hender (Mitt klima— Myclimate Norway).

More practically, NGOs have contributed to opportunities for climate gas compensations. In 2006 Norges Naturvernforbund launched an internet homepage where individuals and private households can calculate their emissions and buy compensation (www.klimakutt.no, accessed 18 March 2009). For business companies and organisations, an opportunity to compensate for travel emissions is established in a cooperation between Norges Naturvernforbund, the travel agency HRG Nordic Grimstad and GRID-Arendal (the office of the United Nations Environmental Programme in Norway). The revenue from compensation purchases is used for, for example, energy-saving projects in Central Asia, the Caucasus and Eastern Europe. The climate gas compensation systems are thus extending the activities of NGOs. The organisation Mitt klima offers 'climate tickets' to consumers as well as a service for travel agencies and business companies to offer climate compensation and environmental information to travellers (www.mittklima.no, accessed 18 March 2009). Seven travel agencies are involved in this scheme.

The idea of calculating and keeping account of climate gas emissions from individual air travel does not originate from governments or airline companies but seems to have appeared primarily among environmental NGOs, scientists and concerned individuals. For several years there have been calculation tools available, for example on the internet, and the knowledge base behind these calculations has developed. In recent years, the feature of being able to calculate environmental costs and to buy compensation has been added to a number of these offers. The CarbonNeutral Company, which is currently delivering a CO_2 calculation service to SAS, Widerøe and other airline companies in Norway, grew out of a cooperation between NGO-active people and scientists and was originally, in 1997, named Future Forests.

The price of climate compensation for a journey is typically around 25–200 NKR (around €3–23). The amount is, compared with the price of an aeroplane ticket, relatively small. The ticket prices vary widely; however, for ordinary economy-class tickets the climate gas compensation represents perhaps between 2% and 8% of the ticket price.

In 2007 the climate impact of air travel was a subject frequently described in the Norwegian mass media. General public awareness and discussion about human-made climate change have increased in recent years. Concerns about the changes are evident, for example, in everyday conversations and media pieces about the weather, the lack of snow for skiing and threats to Norwegian nature and wildlife (such as to polar bears in the arctic areas). Surveys showed a significant increase in consumer awareness about the environmental impacts of travel in the months immediately following the government's launch of its climate compensation scheme. Some 47% of those surveyed stated that they have become more engaged and aware of the environmental issues as a result of the increased public discussion and media coverage of the climate subject.

Many airline passengers indicate that they support the climate gas compensation scheme. In a survey among charter passengers, around 30% indicated that they will buy compensation the next time they travel by air; 11.3% stated that they had done so on their latest journeys. Some 75% agreed that 100 NKR is a suitable amount to pay as compensation (Furuly 2007).

Similar figures for business customers are not available; however, a survey covering 1,300 Norwegian companies shows that, though environmental aspects are not the highest prioritised issue in connection with travel, about 15% of those persons responsible for companies' travel say that they will in future consider environmental aspects more. A number of business companies have announced that they will buy climate gas compensation for their air travel. Among these is the large oil company Statoil. Also, a number of interest-group organisations—for example, the Norwegian association of consultants—have announced such business policy. Also, SAS itself has decided that its employees' travel will be CO_2 compensated. Travel agencies have experienced demand from business and private customers for climate gas compensation and have in a number of instances established opportunities for doing so.

4.1.3 Critical views

Despite support from many sides to the climate gas compensation scheme, there is considerable discussion and disagreement about it when seen as a strategy for reduced climate impacts and sustainable consumption. It is pointed out that such schemes have important limitations.

Generally, it is questioned whether the scheme will lead to a substantial change in climate gas emissions or in the demand for air flight mobility. Many find compensation and emission trading a rather indirect way of addressing the problem of climate-change emissions. The first direct effect will probably be that a greater sum of money is available for investments in climate protection projects in areas other than air traffic and for organisations carrying out such projects. Consumers that expect a direct reduction in the climatic impacts of travel may in many cases feel a bit cheated and find the carbon compensation opportunity disappointing and with quite uncertain outcome. Similarly, many find it wrong to refer to compensated travel as 'climate-friendly' and think that compensation schemes are a step away from principles of letting the polluters be responsible for cleaning up the pollution.

Critics have advanced the view that climate gas compensation is a way of buying indulgences. The following quote shows this view and, moreover, shows that climate has also become an issue in the popular media (it appeared in an in–out list in the lifestyle and entertainment section of a newspaper in Denmark). Number three on the In! list:

> Indulgence. CO_2 credits. Such certificates for reduced CO_2 pollution, that private individuals, companies and the state buy in the development countries, because we do not feel like cleaning up our own shit. Such a condescending idea, that one has to take off one's hat (Dahlager 2007; author's translation).

Professional analysts have also argued that it can be an indirect way of addressing the problems. Moreover, it is pointed to that a market for greenhouse gas emissions is an artificial and imaginary construction that does not always make sense, economically speaking, to people and is a considerable bureaucratic challenge (E24 2007). There are discussions about the practical workings of such an economic emission compensation scheme where emissions are priced in a tradable way. The efficiency that economists have claimed for such markets may be overrated, and the practical problems and costs of developing and operating the markets are considerable. For Norway this was, for example, experienced in the collapse in 2007 of plans for a common Swedish and Norwegian market for 'green' certificates in the energy sector.

Environmental NGOs have criticised the climate gas compensation scheme and other efforts made by the government for not being sufficient to make a significant impact on climate change and for not being sufficient as a climate policy.

The voluntary character of the scheme (to others than the state administration) is pointed out as an important weak point.

In addition, within the Norwegian government and parliament there have been disagreements over the climate gas compensation scheme as a key point of climate policy. Critical opinions put forward are that the scheme and other suggested efforts are not sufficiently ambitious to make Norway a leading country in the field. Rather, it is suggested, it appears as a laggard primarily, following after developments internationally and in the EU.

4.2 Results

The climate gas compensation scheme in Norway has resulted in considerable awareness of the impacts of climate-change gases created by air travel and the need to limit such emissions. This increased awareness has been apparent among consumers in general, in media discussions and on the policy agenda. The extended media coverage covers not only general mass media for the broad population but also more specific media for travellers and professionals within the air traffic sector. In the period 2001–2003 there were almost no such articles—today they are very frequent.

The compensation scheme has, moreover, supported airline companies and travel agencies in introducing systems for buying compensation in connection with the purchase of travel tickets. The scheme has indicated a demand for such systems. More generally, the compensation scheme has signalled support to actors in the air transport sector in their development of strategies for handling climate problems.

Internationally, the compensation scheme has sent a signal to governmental leaders and the EU that Norway supports reinforced efforts against climate-change emissions from air travel and that it thinks that governments and public authorities should play an active and leading role in such efforts.

The climate gas compensation scheme has resulted in a boost in the sale of climate compensation through channels established by NGOs. In the first 12 months, Mitt klima sold to private individuals 2,500 climate tickets for 550,000 NKR, many of them in the period immediately after the government's announcement of the compensation scheme. In the first five months Norges Naturvernforbund sold compensation to around 700 persons for around 300,000 NKR, equalling 1,500 tons CO_2. Kirkens Nødhjælp has sold compensation to a value of around 50,000 NKR. In total, the three NGOs sold compensations for around 900,000 NKR to private consumers and households (Larsen 2007).

Within the first two months of the offer, on the SAS internet homepage about 500 passengers used the carbon compensation opportunity. A considerably larger number of users are expected when the opportunity can also be used by business companies and travel agencies and not only through online purchases.

In the period before and after the launch of the climate gas compensation scheme a considerable number of cooperative agreements between providers of compensation management and travel agencies and airline companies were established. One of the results of the climate gas compensation scheme is thus that it has also contributed to making the compensation service, to some degree, a well-established activity and business area.

There are no clear signs of significant changes in the use of air transport as a direct result of the Norwegian climate gas compensation scheme for public employees. At the time of this analysis, the strategy had been in operation for only five months, and figures from the public administrations' actual use of climate gas compensation were not available. The intention of the scheme is that the results will appear primarily through the indirect effects, when other organisations follow and adapt similar strategies.

4.3 Learning experiences and conclusions

The climate gas compensation scheme for Norwegian state employees is an effort to address the climate impacts of air mobility at a societal level. It relates to mass market consumption and is thus more far-reaching than more limited projects and small-scale experiments. Through the intention of interaction with a multitude of actors involved with the issue a system-level perspective is employed. The system-level perspective also appears through its inclusion in general climate policy. The scheme has contributed to putting the climate impacts of air mobility clearly on the societal agenda. With the scheme it has become more normal and acceptable to consider the climate impacts of one's air travel.

Though they can be counted in thousands, the number of consumers buying climate gas compensation is still limited compared with the total number of journeys by air, which are counted in millions. If the carbon compensation opportunity becomes more routinely embedded in procedures for air ticket purchases the penetration of carbon compensation for private users could be much greater. For the moment it is a relatively complicated procedure for consumers.

Though voluntary in principle, a practice that makes routine economic compensation for carbon emissions and makes it the default choice for consumers that do not actively say no to compensation could lead to a larger dissemination of the scheme.

There seems to be great potential in looking to commit business consumers and organisations as a whole, rather than individuals, to compensation. Today, many 'green accounts' held by companies and organisations do not include climate gas emissions arising from the business travel. The establishment of the practice and the routines of climate gas compensation in connection with air flights might facilitate an easy inclusion of this parameter into such accounts. In the long run this could form an important element in efforts towards sustainable mobility within business.

The price of climate compensation for an airplane journey is, as mentioned, typically between 25 and 200 NKR; an amount that, compared with the prices of air tickets, is relatively small and perhaps equals between 2% and 8% of the ticket price. The costs are much smaller than the general reductions in the price of air travel witnessed in the past 10–15 years (Sandberg 2007; Transportøkonomisk institutt 2006). The economic incentive cannot alone be expected to considerably reduce the number of journeys by air when seen in the context of substantial increases in such travel in recent years.

For development in the direction of sustainable mobility there are clearly limitations to the concept of climate gas compensation schemes. Compensation is not synonymous with reduction or, for that case, elimination of climate gas emissions from air travel. The environmental results of compensation schemes appear indirectly, primarily through the schemes for which the compensation money is used. Climate gas compensation schemes are not a sufficient means for creating sustainable consumption, nor are they a solution to problems. However, as pointed out by, for example, representatives of the environmental NGO Friends of the Earth, such schemes are better than nothing.

References

Boarding.no (2007a) 'SAS Braathens vil selge "klimabilletter" ', Boarding.no (Oslo), January 2007.

—— (2007b) 'Widerøe blir litt grønnere', Boarding.no (Oslo), January 2007.

Dahlager, L. (2007) 'Listen, (the "In!" Part)', Politiken, 11 May 2007: section I Byen (Copenhagen: Politikens Hus).

E24 (2007) Köp av ratter minskar inte utsläppen (Stockholm: E24 Näringsliv [Svenska Dagbladet]).

EC (European Commission) 2006: Climate Change: Commission Proposes Bringing Air Transport into EU Emissions Trading Scheme (IP/06/1862; Brussels: EC).

EEA (European Environment Agency) (2009) 'Transport at a Crossroads. TERM 2008: Indicators Tracking Transport and Environment in the European Union' (Copenhagen: European Environment Agency; www.eea.europa.eu).

Finstad, A., K. Flugsrud and K. Rypdal (2002) Utslipp til luft fra norsk luftfart (Emissions to Air from Norwegian Air Traffic) (Oslo: Statistics Norway).

Furuly, J.G. (2007) 'Charterturister tenker på miljøet', Aftonposten, Reise, 2 May 2007 (Oslo: Aftonposten and Forbruker.no; www.aftonposten.no).

Hammer, A.S. (2007) 'Får ros for klimakvoter på flyreiser', *Dagsavisen*, 2 January 2007; www.dagsavisen.no (building on figures from Statsministerens kontor).

Larsen, F. (2007) 'Svikter grønne reiser', *Aftonposten, Reise*, 7 May 2007 (Oslo: Aftonposten and Forbruker.no; www.aftonposten.no).

Sandberg, T. (2007) 'Foreslår varig lavpris i lufta', *Dagsavisen* 150307 (Oslo; www.dagsavisen. no, accessed 18 March 2009).

Stoltenberg, J. (2007) *Statsministerens nyttårstale 2007* (Oslo: Statsministerens kontor).

Tajet, G. (2006) *Flytrafikk og miljø (Airplane Traffic and Environment)* (Oslo: Fremtiden i våra hender).

Transportøkonomisk institutt (2006) *The Influence of Competition on Prices of Air Transport* (Oslo: Transportøkonomisk institution).

5
Madrid's high-occupancy vehicle lanes

Theo Geerken

Flemish Institute for Technological Research (VITO), Belgium

Since the 1980s citizens have been moving to the outskirts of Madrid where land prices are still affordable and living in residential areas could be combined with working in the city centre. The population in the city centre remained more or less stable from 1975 (3.2 million) to 2005 (3.1 million). At the outskirts of Madrid, still belonging to the metropolis, the population grew from 1.1 million to 2.8 million in the same period (Pradillo 2006). This rapid urban sprawl, which happened also in many other metropoles (EEA 2006), has created unsustainable effects such as daily congestion for commuting citizens, as road and public transport infrastructure could not be created fast enough and space for widening highways was also limited. Population was growing rapidly in the suburbs, especially along a corridor from Madrid city centre to the northwest.

The high-occupancy vehicle (HOV) lanes in Madrid are Europe's first successful implementation of such lanes, after failure of the HOV lane in Amsterdam. In the USA several thousands of miles of HOV lanes are in use.

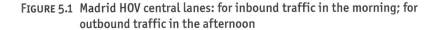

FIGURE 5.1 Madrid HOV central lanes: for inbound traffic in the morning; for outbound traffic in the afternoon

5.1 Case description

5.1.1 Overview

The Madrid HOV lanes were introduced in 1995 in an attempt to reduce conges-tion problems by creating two HOV lanes that are accessible only to buses and cars with two or more persons travelling. The lanes are located as central and bidirectional lanes, allowing them to be used in the morning towards Madrid city centre (inbound traffic; Fig. 5.1) and in the afternoon towards the outskirts (out-bound traffic) and have a length of 12.3 km (HOV) plus the last 3.8 km near the city centre for buses only. The bus-only lane connects the HOV lane to an inter-change point that connects with public transport modes such as the metro, urban buses and suburban buses.

The main objectives were to:

● Reduce travel time by reducing congestion problems by stimulating car pooling and promoting the use of buses

- Increase the road transport capacity

- Reduce environmental impacts

- Increase service quality

A new and flexible infrastructure has been created to induce a behavioural change among commuters. One could characterise this as a systemic change, as changes have occurred in physical infrastructure, public transport services and individuals' travel behaviour. The project was driven top-down by several involved authorities. Travellers are evidently still free to choose between the bus and car and are also free to choose the normal lanes (with usually high congestion levels at rush hour) or the HOV lanes, which provide a shorter travel time. The police check the occupancy of the cars from time to time. A traffic management system informs users about the operation mode and copes with accidents.

5.1.2 Case context: landscape and regime

5.1.2.1 Landscape factors

Important landscape factors that strongly influence the problematic commuting trends related to this case are:

- An increasing number of (double-income) households

- Urban sprawl: people living at the outskirts of a metropolis and working in the city centre

The size of households (in terms of persons per household) is decreasing continuously, leading to the need for more and more homes, whereas the prices of homes in cities are increasing more rapidly than is available income. This leads to so-called urban sprawl, where new living areas are created outside city centres at greater distances from the city centre. As many workplaces are still located in city centres, this leads to more intense traffic patterns for commuters—in the morning rush hour towards the city centre, in the afternoon out of the city centre.

Another important landscape factor (also in the literal sense) is that there was no possibility of creating many more lanes on the highways because of the green areas that need to be protected; also, too many existing homes would need to be destroyed.

5.1.2.2 Sociotechnical regime

The sociotechnical regime that allowed the transport system in Western society to grow over the past century can be characterised by three main players.

- Authorities are responsible for providing and maintaining the public infrastructure for transport (although railway companies often started as private companies), including all associated regulation. Authorities or public bodies are usually also responsible for the operation of public transport. Recently, the concept of privatisation as a means to increase competition and improve service levels has been introduced in the public transport sector. In recent years private investments in public infrastructure have been encouraged by public authorities, most probably to reduce public investment levels

- Private producers of vehicles (cars, trains, buses, etc.) are free to develop and sell vehicles to customers such as consumers, companies and authorities

- Users choose the best solution in terms of budget, time, quality and comfort for their own transport needs or wants

Evidently, private producers of vehicles have to meet the regulations imposed by authorities, such as those relating to safety and to polluting emissions. The transport needs that people have are not a directly controllable issue for authorities, as we are living in a 'free world' and a free-market economy. Indirectly, authorities influence the people's transport needs by, for instance, spatial planning policies relating to living areas and economic activities, or by influencing price levels.

Public transport infrastructure has the character of a public good to be freely used by everybody as long as they pay for it through direct taxes or tickets per usage.

Supportive factors for the fast realisation of the HOV lanes were the increasing nuisance caused by traffic jams and the coming into power of a new political majority.

In The Netherlands an experiment with similar car-pool lanes near Amsterdam in the 1990s has failed, for legal reasons (Van den Bergh *et al.* 2007), where it appeared to be impossible to restrict the use of a public road to cars with more than one occupant.

5.1.3 Actors and their roles and perspectives

The main primary actor that decided to build this new type of infrastructure was the Ministry of Public works, which is part of the central government. Metropolitan transport services (except for the trains) are the responsibility of the local and regional governments, and these actors played a key role in the operation of the new type of infrastructure.

5.1.3.1 Primary actors

There were several actors needed to introduce and operate the HOV lanes (Pozueta Echavarri 1997):

● The Department of Intermodal Planning of Transport in Big Cities, part of the Ministry of Public Works and Transport, was the initiator of the project, even though its own budget was very low

● The Department of Roads, also part of the Ministry of Public Works and Transport, was the main executor and financer of the infrastructure

● The Traffic Department, which belongs to the Ministry of Internal Affairs, is responsible for the exploitation of the roads, to regulate their use

● The Community of Madrid is responsible for the construction of the intermodal interchange point to connect the HOV lane with other means of transport

● The regional transport consortium (a joint initiative between the City and the Community of Madrid) was responsible for the planning of interurban buses

5.1.3.2 Secondary actors and externally involved parties

The potential users of this new type of infrastructure were consulted only after the decision to build the infrastructure was taken already, so that they could influence only the conditions for operation (Pozueta Echavarri 1997). An enquiry by telephone revealed that the majority (about 70%) was positive about the project; 40% expected to use the HOV lane frequently and 60% was willing to consider sharing the use of a car with other people under the condition that the search for contacts would be simple and organised by somebody else.

This relatively late consultation of potential frequent users is a clear deviation from the US manuals on how to create public support for the introduction of HOV lanes, which clearly state that an information campaign beforehand is very important (Van Luven 1995). Apparently, in the Madrid case this omission has been without negative consequences.

5.1.4 Case history and development

The idea of HOV lanes was definitely not new in the world. In the USA the number of miles of HOV lanes has increased since the 1980s to several thousand miles today, usually in the suburban areas of big cities. In 1994 the Seventh National Conference on High-occupancy Vehicle Systems showed its wide acceptance across the USA, although negative criticism has always been around (Van Luven 1994).

In Europe the first HOV lane was constructed in 1991 near Amsterdam, but it has failed for legal reasons (Van den Bergh *et al*. 2007)—apparently because of the impossibility according to Dutch law of restricting use to vehicles with more than one occupant. The first day after its introduction the former minister of transport provoked a fine by driving on the HOV lane alone, to clarify the legal aspects. The HOV lanes near Madrid were the second such lanes in Europe when constructed in 1995 and have operated successfully since then. Other cities have followed, such as Leeds (UK) and Trondheim (Norway).

In the Madrid project all the primary actors have cooperated in a very efficient way to create and put into operation the HOV lanes (Pozueta Echavarri 1997). A committee with representatives from all actors has convened only a number of times without even formal voting rules. Its successful cooperation was probably a result of a new political era that had just started. All authorities are under continuous pressure from voters to solve the problems of congestion and other negative aspects of transport such as noise and poor air quality. In the case of Madrid the traffic jams were at such an unacceptable level that the need for joint action was evident to everybody, which has led to the fast development of the project. It can be stated that the shared sense of urgency has favoured the change. The main 'hot' issue where consensus was not easy to achieve in the committee was the minimum number of occupants per car needed to make use of the HOV lane. Should this be two or three occupants? With two occupants as a minimum there was a risk that the success could be so high that congestion would occur on the HOV lanes, which would lead to criticism and rejection of the system. The fact that human behaviour is relatively unpredictable and the fact that the infrastructure has in some sense a rigid character (two lanes, separated by concrete walls from the other normal lanes) is a risky combination that could lead to it being a victim of its own success. With a minimum of three occupants there exists the risk that few cars would use the HOV lanes, which could lead to the so-called 'empty-lane syndrome': the impression that a piece of infrastructure is badly used might also lead to heavy criticism and rejection of the system. In the end the decision about the minimum number of occupants was taken by another planning department and fixed at two occupants. At the weekend the use of the HOV lane is free to all users (in one direction) as traffic intensity is lower at the weekend and car occupancy is already higher than during the week for obvious reasons such as the higher incidence of family trips at that time.

5.2 Results

5.2.1 Main results

The transport capacity of the road has increased significantly and the transport volume has increased by more than a factor of 1.5 (two additional lanes to the existing four lanes) since the introduction of the HOV lanes (Pradillo 2006).

During the morning rush hours (7 am to 10 am) in 1991, before the HOV lanes existed, some 28,000 commuters were transported in 16,000 vehicles on four normal lanes, already causing traffic jams. In 2005, 52,100 commuters are transported in 25,300 vehicles on four normal lanes and two HOV lanes. The transport volume on the two HOV lanes is 31,700 commuters, which is even higher than the transport volume of 20,400 on the four normal lanes, whereas the HOV lanes still offer a time advantage of 25–43% during morning peak hours (Monzon 2003).

The modal split between cars and buses showed a permanent increase favouring the use of buses during the first ten years of operation. In 1991, before the HOV lane, between 7 am and 10 am 17.1% of the commuters travelled by bus and 55.6% by car (27.3% by train). In 2005, 27.4% travelled by bus, 47.9% by car and 24.7% by train. In addition, the car occupancy has increased from 1.3 in 1991 to 2.0 on the HOV lanes and has decreased to 1.07 on the normal lanes. The bus occupancy on the HOV lanes in 2005 is 31.3, which is much higher than on the normal lanes, with 15.4 passengers, most probably because of the travel time advantage.

The time saving obtained by using the HOV lanes instead of using the normal lanes varies according to the hour, but is about 6–15 minutes on a trip of typically 10–30 minutes (EU CAPTURE Project 1999). Also, the normal lanes are experiencing shorter travel times compared with the situation before the HOV lanes. This also has engendered support from users of the normal lanes.

5.2.2 Change in sustainability performance

The EU CAPTURE Project (1999) made a calculation for the energy use of the car use between 1991 and 1997 in terms of megajoules per passenger kilometre, which showed a 36% decrease as a result of higher car occupancy.

Clearly, the additional land use that these reversible lanes exert is a little over half of that used in the traditional solution of providing extra lanes in both directions. The concrete barriers separating the HOV lanes clearly from the normal lanes need some additional space, but the reversible character saves a factor of two.

Another indirect land-use issue is the impact that the existence of the HOV lane has on the land-use system on a wider scale—it might increase the attractiveness of the living zones that are now more easily accessible (Pfaffenbichler and Mateos 2005). This is a general trend in transport improvements and investments in infrastructure: at their introduction they create benefits through modal shift or efficiency gains, but later on the transport volume increases because of the attractiveness of the new infrastructure.

Solving or reducing Madrid's congestion problems reduced environmental emissions, created social benefits from the 30% time saving and created economic benefits by the reduction of lost working hours of commuters and truck drivers who otherwise are all caught in the same traffic jam.

5.2.3 Learning experiences

- The chain is as strong as its weakest component. It has proven very important that the HOV lane and the piece of bus-only lane connect perfectly to a public transport interchange point to maintain fully the attractive travel time advantage. Maybe this also explains the strong increase in the number of bus users and the relatively small increase in car poolers. If the final destination in the morning of a user is much further than the end of the HOV lane the car poolers continue to lose time later in the trip

- No pain, no change. The experienced sense of urgency has been a very supportive factor for the speed of the process of implementation

- A new team with a new spirit is favourable for change and rapid progress. The new political majority probably favoured a cooperative spirit

- To get people out of the car one really needs an attractive alternative—time-saving and cost-saving buses (including good connections)

- Increased car pooling contributed to the increased road capacity much less than the increased use of buses: car pooling with only family members seems more easy to organise than car pooling with other people

- Important attention points for HOV lanes are: fraud (use with just one driver), accidents on the two HOV lanes, which are separated by concrete walls, and the limited number of entry and exit points

5.3 Potential for diffusion and scaling up

In Madrid the HOV lanes have proven to be able to increase the transport capacity of a lane, especially through the more intense use of buses. The contribution of the additional car poolers has been less significant. In 2005 the central government proposed the creation of approximately 100 km of two-way bus lanes on all radial highways (Javier Barroso 2005).

The potential for bidirectional HOV lanes in general is evidently greatest in larger metropoles with a lot of urban sprawl where massive movements of people during rush hours occur at the radial axes and where there is limited space to widen the highways.

An upcoming question is why only a few European big cities have followed the example of Madrid up to now.

The basic conceptual idea of these bidirectional HOV lanes compared with the ordinary regime is that they use the existing infrastructure more efficiently by creating a flexible and more collective use of a usually rigid infrastructure. Maybe there are other (need) areas where this general idea of flexible infrastructure adapting to the varying intensity of societal needs could be used.

5.4 Overall conclusions

The Madrid HOV lanes have proven to be a success in reducing congestion problems that have arisen from rapid urban sprawl and limited available space for solutions. The transport volume, expressed in terms of the number of passengers, on the two HOV lanes is much higher than on the other four ordinary lanes but still offers a time-saving benefit for those on the HOV lanes.

It has proven to be easier to move people from car to the bus than to increase the level of car pooling. The good connections for public transport located at the end of the HOV lane might explain this fact.

All three sustainability dimensions have benefited from these HOV lanes, the investments are financed by the state and the benefits are received by the users.

Leeds (UK) and Trondheim (Norway) have followed suit in Europe; where will the next examples be?

References

EEA (European Environment Agency) (2006) *Urban Sprawl in Europe: The Ignored Challenge* (Copenhagen: EEA).

EU CAPTURE Project (1999) *Deliverable 8*; ftp.cordis.europa.eu/pub/transport/docs/summaries/urban_capture_report.pdf, accessed 13 July 2009.

Javier Barroso, F.(2005) 'Fomento construirá 120 kilómetros de carriles bus en las autovías de entrada en la capital, Madrid', *El Pais*, 17 March 2005.

Monzon, A. (2003) 'Integrated Policies for Improving Modal Split in Urban Areas', in *Proceedings of the 16th ECMT Symposium, Budapest* (ECMT Publishing): 399-422.

Pfaffenbichler, P., and M. Mateos (2005) 'Location and Transport Effects of High Occupancy Vehicle and Bus Lanes in Madrid', paper presented at the 45th Congress of the European Regional Science Association, Amsterdam, 23–27 August 2005; www-sre.wu-wien.ac.at/ersa/ersaconfs/ersa05/papers/144.pdf, accessed 13 July 2009.

Pozueta Echavarri, J. (1997) 'Experiencia Española en carriles de alta ocupación', in *La calzada BUS/VAO en la N-VI: Balance de un año de funcionamiento* (Madrid: Cuadernos de Investigación Urbanistica, Escuela Técnica Superior de Arquitecture; www.aq.upm.es/Departamentos/Urbanismo/public/ciu/pdf/ciu16/ciu16.pdf , accessed 13 July 2009).

Pradillo, J.M. (2006) 'La Calzada BUS-VAO: Plataformas reservados al transporte público', presentation, Valencia, 3 October 2006; www.cit.gva.es/fileadmin/conselleria/images/Documentos/transportes/jornada/bus-vao.pdf, accessed 13 July 2009.

Van den Bergh, J., E. van Leeuwen, F. Oosterhuis, P. Rietveld and E. Verhoef (2007) 'Social Learning by Doing in Sustainable Transport Innovations: Ex-post Analysis of Common Factors behind Successes and Failures', *Research Policy* 36: 247-59.

Van Luven, H.F. (1995) 'Implementation of HOV Lanes on I-270: Lessons Learned', *Transportation Research Circular* 442 (July 1995).

6

Moving car commuters to public transport in Copenhagen
Appeals to consumer responsibility and improving structural conditions as a means to promote sustainable consumer behaviour

John Thøgersen

University of Aarhus, Denmark

Currently, there is a trend in consumer policy towards assigning increased responsibility to private consumers for the environmental side-effects of their consumption activities (Reisch 2004). This trend is spurred by the observation that environmental side-effects are increasingly generated in the consumption and disposal phases, and to a decreasing extent in the production phase, of the life-cycles of goods and services. As this means that consumer choices and activities at least potentially contribute more to the overall environmental impacts of the production-and-consumption system, it seems natural to assign increasing responsibility to consumers (e.g. see Hansen and Schrader 1997).

However, it needs to be acknowledged that consumers, as individuals, have limited opportunities and abilities to make environmentally beneficial choices (e.g. see Thøgersen 2005b). Hence, if policy-makers put too heavy an emphasis on consumer responsibility without improving structural conditions, which limit consumers' abilities or opportunities to live up to this responsibility, policy-makers are guilty of 'blaming the victims' (Roberts and Bacon 1997). As argued by several scholars, changing structural conditions ('upstream' solutions; see Andreasen 2006; Verplanken and Wood 2006) is usually more effective than interventions targeting consumer beliefs or attitudes (Gardner and Stern 1996; Stern *et al.* 1997). Obviously, consumers' influence on structural conditions, which facilitate or impede sustainable consumption, is indirect (as voters) at best.

Environmentalists have long advocated the view that individual consumers should take responsibility for their acts (e.g. Leopold 1953) as expressed, for instance, in the catchphrase 'think globally, act locally'[1] as well as in the publication of various 'green consumer guides' (e.g. Elkington and Hailes 1989). Others, especially on the political left, emphasised external and personal constraints, which act as barriers on consumers who want to clean up their acts (this is the predominant view, for example, in Goodwin *et al.* 1997). According to this view, companies providing goods and services and governments providing infrastructure, regulating the price structure through taxes and subsidies and setting the general 'rules of the game' through legal standards and other laws and regulations are the primary actors responsible for negative environmental side-effects of consumption.

Most consumer policy scholars (and many practitioners) have traditionally sided with the latter view and pardoned consumers for the negative environmental side-effects of their acts. They have tended to perceive consumers as pawns in a game played by industry and governments: that is, as victims rather than villains. However, there are signs of change in these views. For instance, German consumer policy scholars Hansen and Schrader (1997) suggested that there is a need to modernise the consumer model as a response to the large and growing contribution of private consumption to environmental problems. On the practitioner side, the need for all parties (including consumers) to take responsibility for the sustainability of consumption was voiced strongly at the UN World Summit in Rio in 1992 (Sitarz 1994) and at a number of focused follow-up meetings (e.g. Norwegian Ministry of Environment 1994). According to these practitioners and scholars, it is high time that consumers assume co-responsibility for the negative environmental side-effects of their decisions and behaviour.

Not surprisingly, environmental policy-makers welcome this view. For example, the current Danish administration in 2005 launched a 'Green Responsibility' campaign with the specific objective of strengthening consumers' feeling of personal responsibility for avoiding or cleaning up environmental impacts of

---

1 According to Wikipedia (en.wikipedia.org/wiki/Think_Globally,_Act_Locally), some attribute the expression to the founder of Friends of the Earth, David Brower, who reportedly coined it as the slogan for the organisation when it was founded in 1969, whereas others give the credit to the advisor to the United Nations Conference the on Human Environment in 1972, René Dubois.

consumption.[2] Another example is the European Commission's current 'You Control Climate Change' campaign.[3]

As already mentioned, scholars and practitioners increasingly view campaigns such as these as a natural and necessary component of environmental regulation in a time where private consumption is responsible for a large and increasing share—and industrial production for a decreasing share—of environmental pollution. However, others view these campaigns as just another manifestation of the old observation that when a social problem is put on the agenda the spontaneous response by policy-makers is usually an information campaign targeted at those hurt by the problem, implying that they are responsible for the problem (e.g. Salmon 1989).

Few question that private consumption in the rich parts of the world is unsustainable or that its negative environmental impacts need to be reduced. The controversy on this matter is (by and large) limited to how the problem should and can be most effectively solved.[4] In this perspective, a key question is which of the following is the most important limiting factor for achieving a sustainable consumption pattern: (a) the extent to which consumers assume responsibility for their acts or (b) structural conditions determined by industry and governments?[5] This is, of course, an empirical question, but surprisingly little research exists on the question, and relevant research is tentative and indirect only—for instance, evidence suggesting that information alone is rarely an effective means to promote environmentally responsible behaviour (e.g. Thøgersen 2005a) or that structural changes sometimes are (e.g. Gardner and Stern 1996). As yet, there have been few attempts to provide a direct empirical test of the relative importance of (lack of) consumer responsibility and structural conditions as limiting factors for sustainable consumption.

In this chapter, a longitudinal field study in a population whose behaviour needs to change is offered as a contribution to fill this gap. External confounding factors are controlled by including a control group, not influenced by the structural change. By measuring the relevant behaviour before and after an experimentally induced change in an important structural condition, the behavioural effects of altering the structural condition are quantified. The extent to which members of the population assume responsibility for behaving in a sus-

---

2 See www.mim.dk/ministeren/fokus/groentansvar.htm and www.groentansvar.dk (accessed 18 March 2009).

3 See www.climatechange.eu.com (accessed 18 March 2009).

4 There are also disagreements about what is fair in this connection, but I will concentrate on the effectiveness issue here.

5 Making this an either/or question is obviously an oversimplification. In practice, both might be important, and interacting, limiting factors at the same time (e.g. Guagnano et al. 1995). The simplification is used as a means to sharpen the arguments and clarify the problem.

tainable way is measured with a survey instrument and treated as a between-subjects factor.

The studied case is travel-mode choice. Specifically, the behavioural effects are investigated of providing car owners in a metropolitan area with well-developed public transit service a free monthly pass for public transport.

In environmental psychology, it is common to use Schwartz's (1977) norm-activation theory as the theoretical framework for conceptualising individuals 'assuming responsibility' (e.g. Klöckner and Matthies 2004; Nordlund and Garvill 2003; Steg *et al.* 2006; Stern *et al.* 1999; Thøgersen and Ölander 2006). According to Schwartz's norm-activation theory, feelings of responsibility influence behaviour if they are transformed into a personal moral norm for that particular behaviour. Hence, rather than perceived responsibility the study includes a measure of personal moral norms for the studied behaviour.

6.1 Case description

6.1.1 Overview

Because of its local and global environmental impacts, the rapid growth in automotive transportation is a source of increasing concern worldwide (e.g. Bonsall 2000; Cameron *et al.* 2004; Gaffron 2003; Miljø- og Energiministeriet 1999). Person transport makes up the bulk of total transport, and, increasingly and dominantly, private cars are used (e.g. Cameron *et al.* 2004; Miljø- og Energiministeriet 1999). Policy interventions targeting private transport decisions typically aim to change the modal split, preferably moving medium and long trips to public transport and short trips to walking and biking (e.g. Bonsall 2000; Gaffron 2003; Miljø- og Energiministeriet 1999). In this study, the focus is on moving commuters by car to public transport.

By most standards, the greater Copenhagen area is well served by public transport. As a result, only 38% of households in this area own a car (compared with a national average of 54%; Danmarks Statistik 2001). Still, the city experiences increasing congestion problems, especially in the rush hours, as well as serious air pollution from car traffic. Hence, attempts are made to increase commuting by public transport as an alternative to the private car.

In the current study, it was investigated how effective it would be in this respect to offer public transport for free. Of course, price is only one among a number of structural conditions limiting the use of public transport. Other, perhaps even more important, structural conditions are the frequency, speed, comfort and flexibility of public transport relative to the private car (e.g. Polzin and Maggio 2007). Some people live and work in places in which public transport services are too poorly connected to make such transport a real alternative. Others live close enough to work to have no need for motorised transport for the commute. However, given that the cost of a monthly travel card for public transport in the greater Copenhagen area—by far the cheapest option for commuters—is 995 Danish krona (DKK), or €133, the price is still an important structural condition. Furthermore, among the various structural conditions that limit the use of public transport, price is by far the easiest to change, especially in a field experiment.

For the present study, a random sample of car owners in the greater Copenhagen area was drawn and randomly assigned to receive a free monthly travel card or serve as part of the control group. For subjects in each group, the use of public transport for commuting was measured by self-reports before and after the intervention. Hence, it is possible to calculate the effect on car owners' travel mode choices of radically altering the price structure in favour of public transport. However, the study is limited to short-term effects of price change. In the longer run, free public transport might influence car ownership as well as the choice of locations for living and working, both of which might influence the modal split. A short-term intervention, such as the one studied here, does not produce these effects.

6.1.2 Participants

Data were collected by TNS Gallup by means of telephone interviews carried out in October and November 2002. Subjects were a random sample of car owners in the Greater Copenhagen area fulfilling the following screening criteria: they had a driver's licence and a car at their disposal; they commuted to their job or study at least once a week; they were not dependent on a private car to do their job; and they had not held a monthly travel card for public transport in the Greater Copenhagen area for at least a year. If more than one person in the household fulfilled these criteria, the one who had the birthday next was asked to participate in the study.

Of those meeting the screening criteria, 1,071 agreed to participate in the first wave, resulting in a response rate of 75% of those qualifying. Thirty subjects were excluded because letters outlining experiment information were returned by post because of an incorrect address, because they claimed not to have received the information or because of errors in the administration of the experiment during the telephone interview. Owing to panel attrition, the sample size was reduced to 919 in the second round.

The allocation to experiment and control groups followed a somewhat complex design. First, participants were randomly assigned to either the experimental treatment group (70%) or the control group (30%).[6] In the experiment

6 As 30 experimental subjects were excluded, the proportions in the final sample became 69%:31%. The excluded subjects did not differ significantly (at the 5% level) from included subjects on any of the target variables in the first wave.

group, subjects were then assigned to one of several sub-groups. Those expressing any intention to use public transport in the near future were randomly assigned to one of two sub-groups: (a) a planning exercise alone or (b) a planning exercise plus a free monthly travel card. The planning exercise consisted of asking subjects to plan their next trip with public transport (when exactly they would go, their start and end point, using which bus or train connection; see Bamberg 2002).

Those expressing no intention of using public transport in the near future were randomly assigned to one of three sub-groups: (a) a customised timetable alone, (b) a customised timetable plus a free monthly travel card or (c) a free monthly travel card alone. The customised timetable treatment consisted of sending subjects a customised timetable for his or her daily commute based on information about home and work given during the first interview. Free monthly travel cards and customised timetables were sent to participants by ordinary mail immediately after the first interview.

Neither the planning exercise nor the customised timetable produced an increase in commuting by public transport over and above the control group (for details, see Thøgersen and Møller 2007). For this reason, and because the focus here is on the effect of altering the price structure, experimental subjects not receiving a free travel card were excluded from this study. Hence, the final sample consisted of 748 car owners living in the greater Copenhagen area and being in employment or education, who participated in both rounds of this study, serving either as experimental subjects (481, receiving a free monthly travel card) or as members of the control group (267).

The sex distribution of the participants was 51:49 men:women. The average age was 43 years and the age range 18 to 74 years. Some 70% were living with at least one other adult, and 47% had children under the age of 18 years in the household. A total of 50% had a college or university degree; 50% lived in a house, 48% in an apartment and 2% in other types of homes. None of these descriptors differed significantly between the experiment group and the control group.

6.1.3 Measures

In both waves, answers were obtained to questions about the use of public transport for commuting and about moral norms regarding this behaviour, in that order. There were also questions about other issues not pertinent to the present report.

6.1.3.1 Behaviour

The degree of commuting by public transport was measured on a scale from 0 to 10 by the question: 'How many of the last 10 times did you use public transport for the trip between home and work/educational institution?' In the following analyses, answers are coded so that a higher number indicates more frequent behaviour.

6.1.3.2 Moral norms

Each respondent's moral norms were measured by the question: 'How right or wrong is it for you to use public transport for the trip to work/education?' (cf. Manstead 2000). Answers were given on a five-point scale, with the end points being 'very wrong' and 'very right'. Only 11.4% and 14.6% of experimental and control subjects, respectively, answered 'very right', and an additional 7.9% and 7.6%, respectively, answered 'somewhat right'. For the present study, 'very right' responses were coded as 1 (strong moral norm) and all other valid responses were coded as 0 (weak moral norm).

6.1.3.3 Intervention

After completing the first interview, members of the experiment group were mailed a free monthly travel card for public transport (buses and trains) in the Greater Copenhagen area. Hence, for them (but not for the control group) the price structure in the local travel market was radically, albeit only temporarily, altered. The cover letter briefly thanked them for participating in the study and informed them that the free travel card was for personal use only, that it had to be signed and that they had received it based on a random draw among the participants.

6.2 Results

A 2 (receivers of a free travel card compared with the control group) × 2 (weak versus strong moral norm) × 2 (before versus after) mixed between-and-within subjects design is applied to the data, which is analysed by means of general linear modelling (SPSS 13). The mean values are shown graphically in Figure 6.1.

As expected, the pattern of means differs between the receivers of a free travel card and the control group. Among control group subjects, behaviour did not change significantly between the two measurement points ($F = 0.325, p = 0.57$) and the interaction between moral norms and measurement time is also not significant for the control group ($F = 1.098, p = 0.30$). However, there is a direct

FIGURE 6.1 **Use of public transport among car owners in Copenhagen who received a free monthly travel card and control subjects before and after receiving the free travel cards**

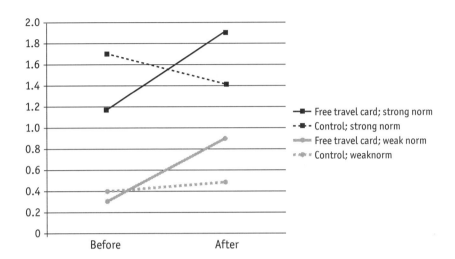

effect seen for moral norms: those with strong moral norms used public transport significantly more than those with weak moral norms ($F = 17.433$, $p < 0.001$).

In the free travel card group, the use of public transport increased significantly between the two measurement points ($F = 15.721$, $p < 0.001$). As in the control group, those with strong moral norms used public transport significantly more than those with weak moral norms ($F = 16.973$, $p \leq 0.001$) and the interaction between moral norms and time of measurement is not statistically significant ($F = 0.111$, $p = 0.74$).

Further, as expected, the use of public transport did not differ between intervention and control group subjects before the intervention, either in the group with weak moral norms ($F = 0.785$, $p = 0.38$) or in the strong moral norm group ($F = 0.709$, $p = 0.40$). At the second measurement point (i.e. during the intervention period), weak moral norm subjects who received a free travel card used public transport significantly more than their control group counterpart ($F = 7.099$, $p < 0.01$). The difference between intervention and control group subjects with strong moral norms was still not significant ($F = 0.626$, $p = 0.43$), but whereas the control group's use of public transport fell the intervention group's increased between the two measurement points. The interaction between experimental condition and time was marginally significant ($F = 2.588$, $p < 0.06$, one-tailed test).

6.3 Discussion

Although it is well known that car traffic is responsible for serious societal and environmental problems and that public transport is widely advocated as a superior alternative, especially for commuting, only a small minority of Copenhagen car owners appear to feel a strong personal responsibility to reduce their car use and thus commute by public transport instead. We can only speculate why, but a likely candidate is that the huge number of cars on the streets not only creates congestion and air pollution but also a descriptive norm supporting car driving (cf. Cialdini *et al.* 1990). Under these conditions, and given that leading members of society, including ministers for the environment, are much more often seen driving cars than in public transport (except aeroplanes!), it is an uphill battle to create a widespread and strong feeling of responsibility to reduce car driving among members of the general public. This is a pity because, according to this study, individual drivers' acceptance of responsibility is the key to a substantial shift in the modal split from private cars to public transport, given facilitating conditions such as those created by the public transport system of the Greater Copenhagen area. Under these conditions, the strength of car owners' moral norms (which mediates the effects of acceptance of responsibility) makes a bigger difference to their use of public transport than does its price (within the rather broad price range explored in this study; i.e. from free to the current price). A campaign that were to move everyone to the strong moral norm group would produce a (slightly) larger increase in the use of public transport (a maximum average effect across the whole sample of 0.97 trips out of 10)[7] than making the service free for all (a short-term effect of 0.70). It is hard to imagine a campaign with this level of success, however. Hence, the 0.97 trips out of 10 should be viewed as a ceiling, not as a realistic target for a campaign aimed at strengthening individual responsibility and moral norms regarding the use of public transport.

Some people live and work in places that are either too badly connected by public transport services to make public transportation a real alternative, or they live so close to work that they have no need for motorised transport for commuting. For these individuals, not only their personal attitudes towards public

---

7 The difference in means between the strong and weak moral norm groups before intervention was 1.1. Since the effect is limited to those with weak moral norms, the average effect across the whole sample is 0.97.

transportation but also the price of using public transport are inconsequential. The only things that could make those served poorly by the current public transport system change their modal split would be either (a) force or (b) radical improvements in the basic service (an extended, faster, more comfortable and/or more flexible public transport service).

For others, the price is an important structural condition, however, as illustrated by this study. By offering public transport for free it was possible to double commuting by public transport (from 0.7 to 1.4 out of 10 trips on average). This is the short-term effect only and, given the high stability of travel mode choices (Thøgersen 2006), it is not a bad result. As the effects of moral norms, this short-term effect is contingent on the level of service provided by the public transport system. Further, as mentioned earlier, it is likely that a radical change in the relative prices of travel options, such as the one produced by offering public transport for free, would influence behaviour more in the longer than in the short run because of the influence on car ownership and the choice of where to live and work.

6.4 Potential for diffusion and scaling up

There is no reason to doubt that environmental policy-makers are generally insightful people who are well aware that consumers, as individuals, have limited opportunities and abilities to make environmentally beneficial choices. However, they may honestly believe (or hope) that there are 'low-hanging fruits' that can be harvested simply by increasing consumer attention towards serious environmental problems and making them more aware of how their choices as consumers can make a difference. This could, for instance, be the case if changes in important structural conditions have been implemented the potential of which has not yet been fully exploited or if new important knowledge has become available that is not yet widely disseminated. Whether there is such an unexploited potential within the given structural conditions, or whether it is necessary to change structural conditions in order to substantially reduce environmental side-effects from consumption, is an empirical question.

In this chapter, a case study of travel-mode choice, carried out in a specific national context, provided evidence pertaining to this question. Specifically, it is explored whether campaigns for increasing consumer responsibility or improving structural conditions hold the biggest potential as a means to promote sustainable consumer behaviour in the area of travel-mode choice. The case studied concerns a key problem area when it comes to the sustainability of consumption and the focal point of attempts to regulate consumer behaviour in most developed countries. In addition, travel-mode choice is a specific behaviour that poses its own specific opportunities and constraints for environmental policy-makers. Whereas some environmentally relevant types of behaviour are carried out in the privacy of one's home, which makes them close to invisible to other people, except visitors in the home, travelling is a public act. Although it may seem paradoxical, this may actually be one of the reasons why only a small minority of car owners feels that they should use public transport instead of the private car for commuting.

Also the specific private cost–benefit structure of the behaviour matters, of course. Use of public transport definitely has private side-benefits, such as opportunities to read and relax. At the costs side, use of public transport can extend daily commuting time by an hour or more in the Copenhagen area, in addition to the effort of walking to and from the bus or train and needing to adjust clothing to weather conditions.

When it comes to increasing consumer responsibility, the unexploited potential obviously differs substantially between environmentally relevant types of behaviour. For example, the potential seems relatively high for travel mode choices. However, the ease or difficulty of changing perceptions of responsibility also differs between different types of behaviour. For instance, the public nature of travelling, combined with mode choices predominantly favouring the private car, means that communication aiming at creating a normative pressure for using alternatives to the private car competes with the much stronger voice of thousands of car drivers' everyday choices (Kallgren *et al.* 2000). Hence, it is probably no coincidence that consumers' felt responsibility is so low for this particular behaviour. Indeed, increasing consumers' felt responsibility for making sustainable travel-mode choices is probably far from a 'low-hanging fruit'. Further, it is doubtful anyone expects it to be equally easy to convince everybody that they have a responsibility for the environmental side-effects of their consumer choices. Some can be convinced by good arguments, others are more reluctant and need to see many others take responsibility before they will do it themselves, and some are neither persuaded by arguments nor by modelling. Hence, in areas where the level of felt responsibility is already high, it may be quite costly to extend it even further.

It has not been the objective of this study to evaluate campaigns aimed at increasing consumer responsibility. Instead, the objective was to quantify the maximum behavioural effects (i.e. ceiling) that campaigners could hope for if they were to succeed in making consumers assume more responsibility (or, more precisely, in making more consumers assume responsibility) for environmental harm caused by their actions. Rather than considering the many things that can go wrong in such a campaign, this study has focused on the behavioural effects if the goals of the campaign were actually reached.

The study presented here suggest that, when the goal is to reduce the environmental side-effects of consumer activities, there may often be more to gain from changing structural conditions to facilitate the desired behaviour. Offering public transport for free doubled commuting by public transport among Copenhagen car owners. The case study points attention to structural conditions that impede consumers' ability or opportunity to make sustainable choices. Among other things, it shows that a majority of car drivers seemingly cannot be persuaded either by moral arguments or by a change in the price structure to change their commuting habits. These are predominantly people whose current commuting needs cannot be met by existing public transport services. If public transport were to be made free on a permanent basis, this might influence decisions about where to buy a home or apply for a job and thereby increase the use of public transport more in the longer term than in the short term. The same effect may be achievable through measures making car driving in the city more expensive, as has been implemented in metropolitan areas such as Singapore, London, Oslo and Stockholm.

Another, or supplementary, option of course is to improve the public transport service to areas with many commuters and a relatively poor service. Other types of behaviour have their own specific impediments to the making of sustainable choices.

Changing structural conditions to be more facilitating for sustainable consumer choices is rarely without cost. However, neither are campaigns aimed at increasing consumer responsibility, and if policy-makers are serious about the goal of sustainable consumption it should count that information campaigns alone have a very bad record when it comes to changing behaviour. The best results have usually been demonstrated in cases where important structural conditions were improved in combination with a well-designed information campaign (e.g. Stern 1999).

For pedagogical reasons, and in order to warn against what I believe is a tendency to overemphasise individual consumer responsibility for solving problems related to unsustainable consumption patterns, I have pitted structural changes against campaigns targeting consumers' responsibility, as if they were alternatives, which they obviously are not. No single instrument is sufficient to meet the huge challenge of achieving a sustainable consumption pattern, as formulated in Agenda 21 (Sitarz 1994) and the follow-up agreements at the UN Johannesburg Summit. Changing public perceptions, as consumers and as voters, is part of the solution as is the need for structural changes that make sustainable choices relatively less costly and unsustainable choices more costly, not only in terms of money but also in terms of time and effort.

6.5 Overall conclusions

This case study illustrates that the extent to which consumers take responsibility and develop personal moral norms for their acts has a significant influence on the sustainability of the consumption pattern and that there are often structural changes that can be made to facilitate sustainability. In the case analysed, it seemed that the potential gains from the studied structural change were of the same order of magnitude as the potential gains from a successful campaign targeting consumer responsibility. In other cases, there may be bigger differences between what can be achieved by the two approaches.

So, should policy-makers in general offer public transport for free? That conclusion cannot be drawn from this study alone. In addition to the financial costs, there could be a number of societal disadvantages in doing so. However, what we can conclude is that the relative prices of the alternative commuting offers matter and that alterations to the price structure to favour public transport relative to the private car could make a substantial contribution to improve the sustainability of this important consumption area.

Campaigns to increase responsible consumer choices in this area are also meaningful, according to the evidence. However, given the historical record it is obvious that this is not an easy goal. As long as the vast majority, including political leaders, prefer to use cars for their transport it is very difficult to establish a feeling of responsibility not to do so among individual consumers. Hence, without structural changes that facilitate a major shift to alternative means of transport, it is hardly possible to improve feelings of responsibility in this area.

References

Andreasen, A. (2006) *Social Marketing in the 21st Century* (London: Sage).

Bamberg, S. (2002) 'Effects of Implementation Intentions on the Actual Performance of New Environmentally Friendly Behaviours: Results of Two Field Experiments', *Journal of Environmental Psychology* 22: 399-411.

Bonsall, P. (2000) 'Legislating for Modal Shift: Background to the UK's New Transport Act', *Transport Policy* 7: 179-84.

Cameron, I., T.J. Lyons and J.R. Kenworthy (2004) 'Trends in Vehicle Kilometres of Travel in World Cities, 1960–1990: Underlying Drivers and Policy Responses', *Transport Policy* 11: 287-98.

Cialdini, R.B., R.R. Reno and C.A. Kallgren (1990) 'A Focus Theory of Normative Conduct: Recycling the Concept of Norms to Reduce Littering in Public Places', *Journal of Personality and Social Psychology* 58: 1,015-26.

Danmarks Statistik (2001) *Familiernes bilrådighed 2001* (Copenhagen: Danmarks Statistik).

Elkington, J., and J. Hailes (1989) *The Green Consumer Guide. From Shampoo to Champagne: High-Street Shopping for a Better Environment* (London: Victor Gollancz).

Gaffron, P. (2003) 'The Implementation of Walking and Cycling Policies in British Local Authorities', *Transport Policy* 10: 235-44.

Gardner, G.T., and P.C. Stern (1996) *Environmental Problems and Human Behaviour* (Boston, MA: Allyn & Bacon).

Goodwin, N.R., F. Ackerman and D. Kiron (1997) *The Consumer Society* (Washington, DC: Island Press).

Guagnano, G.A., P.C. Stern and T. Dietz (1995) 'Influences on Attitude–Behaviour Relationships: A Natural Experiment with Curbside Recycling', *Environment and Behaviour* 27: 699-718.

Hansen, U., and U. Schrader (1997) 'A Modern Model of Consumption for a Sustainable Society', *Journal of Consumer Policy* 20: 443-68.

Kallgren, C.A., R.R. Reno and R.B. Cialdini (2000) 'A Focus Theory of Normative Conduct: When Norms Do and Do Not Affect Behaviour', *Personality and Social Psychology Bulletin* 26: 1,002-12.

Klöckner, C.A., and E. Matthies (2004) 'How Habits Interfere with Norm-Directed Behaviour: A Normative Decision-making Model for Travel Mode Choice', *Journal of Environmental Psychology* 24: 319-27.

Leopold, A. (1953) *A Sand County Almanac: With Essays in Conservation from Round River* (Oxford, UK: Oxford University Press).

Manstead, A.S.R. (2000) 'The Role of Moral Norm in the Attitude–Behaviour Relationship', in D.J. Terry and M.A. Hogg (eds.), *Attitudes, Behaviour, and Social Context: The Role of Norms and Group Membership* (Mahwah: Lawrence Erlbaum): 11-30.

Miljø- og Energiministeriet (1999) *Natur- og miljøpolitisk redegørelse 1999* (Copenhagen: Miljø- og Energiministeriet).

Nordlund, A.M., and J. Garvill (2003) 'Effects of Values, Problem Awareness, and Personal Norm on Willingness to Reduce Personal Car Use', *Journal of Environmental Psychology* 23: 339-47.

Norwegian Ministry of Environment (1994) *Symposium: Sustainable Consumption, Oslo, 19–20 January 1994*.

Polzin, S.E., and E. Maggio (2007) *Public Transit in America: Analysis of Access using the 2001 National Household Travel Survey* (Tampa, FL: National Centre for Transit Research, University of South Florida).

Reisch, L.A. (2004) 'Principles and Visions of a New Consumer Policy', *Journal of Consumer Policy* 27: 1-42.

Roberts, D.A., and D.R. Bacon (1997) 'Exploring the Subtle Relationship between Environmental Concern and Ecological Conscious Consumer Behaviour', *Journal of Business Research* 40: 79-89.

Salmon, C.T. (1989) 'Campaigns for Social "Improvements": An Overview of Values, Rationales, and Impacts', in C.T. Salmon (ed.), *Information Campaigns: Balancing Social Values and Social Change* (Newbury Park, CA: Sage): 19-53.

Schwartz, S.H. (1977) 'Normative Influence on Altruism', in L. Berkowitz (ed.), *Advances in Experimental Social Psychology. Vol. 10* (New York: Academic Press): 221-79.

Sitarz, D. (ed.). (1994) *Agenda 21: The Earth Summit Strategy to Save Our Planet* (Boulder, CO: Earth Press).

Steg, L., L. Dreijerink and W. Abrahamse (2006) 'Factors Influencing the Acceptability of Energy Policies: A Test of VBN Theory', *Journal of Environmental Psychology* 25: 415-25.

Stern, P.C. (1999) 'Information, Incentives, and Pro-environmental Consumer Behaviour', *Journal of Consumer Policy* 22: 461-78.

——, T. Dietz, T. Abel, G.A. Guagnano and L. Kalof (1999) 'A Value–Belief–Norm Theory of Support for Social Movements: The Case of Environmentalism', *Human Ecology Review* 6: 81-97.

——, T. Dietz, V.W. Ruttan, R.H. Socolow and J.H. Sweeney (eds.) (1997) *Environmentally Significant Consumption* (Washington, DC: National Academy Press).

Thøgersen, J. (2005a) 'Consumer Behaviour and the Environment: Which Role for Information?', in S. Krarup and C.S. Russell (eds.), *Environment, Information and Consumer Behaviour* (Cheltenham, UK: Edward Elgar): 51-63.

—— (2005b) 'How May Consumer Policy Empower Consumers for Sustainable Lifestyles?', *Journal of Consumer Policy* 28: 143-78.

—— (2006) 'Understanding Repetitive Travel Mode Choices in a Stable Context: A Panel Study Approach', *Transportation Research Part A: Policy and Practice* 40: 621-38.

—— and B. Møller (2007) 'Breaking Car-Use Habits: The Effectiveness of a Free Month Travel Card', *Transportation* 35: 329-45.

—— and F. Ölander (2006) 'The Dynamic Interaction of Personal Norms and Environment-friendly Buying Behaviour: A Panel Study', *Journal of Applied Social Psychology* 36: 1,758-80.

Verplanken, B., and W. Wood (2006) 'Interventions to Break and Create Consumer Habits', *Journal of Public Policy and Marketing* 25: 90-103.

7

The Munich Dialogue Marketing Campaign for New Citizens

Using residential relocation as a starting point for breaking car use habit

Sebastian Bamberg

University of Applied Science Bielefeld, Germany

This case study reports the development and effects of a marketing campaign aiming to motivate car drivers to use public transport (PT) more frequently for everyday trips in Munich, Germany. The special feature of the campaign lies in the fact that it uses a context change—residential relocation—as a starting point for triggering the desired behavioural change. The campaign was initiated and financed by the marketing department of the public transport company MVG and the local authorities of Munich. The task of our research group consists in providing a theoretical framework of the psychological mechanisms potentially mediating the campaign impact and to conduct the evaluation study. Omniphon, a leading German PT marketing firm, was commissioned with the technical development and implementation of the campaign. The whole project was designed as a large-scale pilot study aiming to test the technical feasibility of the campaign design under real market conditions and to provide data that are as hard as possible concerning the behavioural impact of marketing campaigns targeting movers. For this purpose a true experimental design was used.

7.1 Case description

7.1.1 Theoretical background

Longitudinal studies (e.g. Thøgersen 2006) indicate that car use for everyday trips is a very stable behaviour that is difficult to influence by traditional, 'downstream' interventions such as education or information campaigns that target the individual directly by identifying the costs of car use and the benefits of public transport, cycling or walking. Many researchers (e.g. Aarts *et al.* 1998; Gärling and Axhausen 2003) propose that viewing car use as a prototypical example of a habitual behaviour provides an explanation for the ineffectiveness of traditional information campaigns: habits are conceptualised as a form of automaticity of response that develops as people repeat actions in stable circumstances with rewarding consequences (Verplanken and Aarts 1999). Verplanken and Wood (2006) see at least three reasons why persuasive communication might not be effective in influencing habitual behaviour:

- Habits seem to predispose people to biased processing of information. People with strong habits expect prior experiences to be repeated, and thus they search less for information about behavioural alternatives but for information about the performance context itself. In addition, their search tends to be biased toward confirming the habitual option

- Habit learning is characterised by cognitive and motivational processes in which the control of action is outsourced to the environment so that sequences of prior actions are triggered automatically by the appropriate circumstances

- The automatic activation of habits is probably also the reason why habit performance is so often perpetuated over alternative actions: whole sequences of habitual responses can be automatically activated by the environment and implemented as a unit

In summary, the expectations established through behaviour repetition with satisfying results in a stable context can be seen as conservative forces that reduce openness to new information and that perpetuate well-practised behaviour despite people's intentions to do otherwise.

However, the dependence of habits on stable environmental contexts simultaneously opens an effective way for breaking them: changing the context interrupts the automatically activated association between environmental cues and a specific behavioural pattern. Thus, interventions aiming to change habits should try to pair the traditional downstream interventions with naturally occurring lifestyle changes.

The aim of the Munich project was systematically to evaluate the effectiveness of this downstream-plus-context-change intervention approach in the context of people's daily travel behaviour after a residential move. Some local administrations and public transportation companies (e.g. Bamberg 2006; Bühl 2002; Loose 2004) have already tried to use the time-period after a residential relocation as a 'window of opportunity' for changing new citizens' travel behaviour. Typical elements of these mover marketing campaigns are the provision of a one-week free PT test ticket and PT services-related information as soon as possible after the move. Evaluations of these campaigns indicate these simple measures do have an impact on new citizens' travel behaviour: new citizens receiving the intervention report a substantive increase in use of PT and a corresponding decrease in car use. However, the ability to draw strong causal inferences for these early studies (e.g. Bühl 2002; Loose 2004) is severely limited by the fact that the results are based on research designs with low internal validity: instead of randomised control trials, simple one-group pre–post test designs are used, behavioural change is measured only via retrospective self-reports and low response rates indicate self-selection processes.

Thus the main goal of the present study was to evaluate a theory-based, professionally developed and conducted mover marketing campaign in the context of a research design with high internal (randomised control trial) and external (representative sample) validity.

7.1.2 Description of the marketing campaign

The campaign, the 'Dialogue Marketing Campaign for Munich's New Citizens', was conducted from October 2005 to March 2006. The campaign was based on the following two-step individualised marketing approach (e.g. Bróg *et al.* 2003): after registering at the municipal office (obligatory in Germany) new citizens received the information pack 'München—Gescheid mobil' (Munich—clever mobility) as soon as possible via mail. The information pack contained three elements:

- A personally addressed welcome letter written by the mayor of Munich and the MVG director, already referring to the possibility of requesting a free PT test ticket and listing central mobility-related hotlines, addresses and web pages

- A 30-page professionally styled folder containing central information about the local mobility options: public transport (9 pages), cycling and walking (6 pages), car use and parking (4 pages), distant travelling (3 pages) and the health, environmental, financial and time costs of car use in comparison with PT (7 pages). Also included in the folder was a city map (1:24,000) specially produced for the campaign showing all PT routes and stops as well as a schematic overview plan of Munich's PT routes and tariff information. To secure the usability and attractiveness of the information contained in the folder, prototype versions were tested with representative mover samples and were improved according to comments received

- A so-called 'service card' that could be used to request 16 additional information brochures (e.g. small pocket timetables for specific PT routes, sightseeing in Munich with PT, guides for walking and cycling tours in or around Munich, and so on). The service card also offered the chance to request a free one-week PT pass valid for all PT services in and around Munich (value about €20). Persons who used the service card were asked to provide a phone number

In the second step of the dialogue marketing campaign these phone numbers were used for contacting the new citizens personally, especially those who requested the free ticket. During the phone call the citizens were asked to report their experiences with PT use in Munich, whether they intended to continue using PT and whether they needed additional assistance or information for this purpose. At the end of the conversation they were asked whether they were interested in buying a long-term PT ticket. If they showed interest, an order form was sent to them.

7.1.3 Goals of the evaluation study

The main focus of the evaluation study was on process and outcome evaluation: whereas process evaluation concentrates on the question of whether participants actually receive the campaign elements as intended and how intensely they use these delivered campaign elements, outcome evaluation concentrates on the question of whether the campaign has a measurable impact on the behaviour of interest: in our case travel model choice for daily trips in Munich. An additional goal of the evaluation study was to provide insights into mechanisms mediating or moderating the impact of the marketing campaign. More precisely, we assumed that the anticipated adaptation to an expected change in transport infrastructural conditions at a new place of residence provides an explanation of the observation reported in earlier studies that a move itself, without any intervention, seems to trigger changes in daily travel behaviour. Thus we see the role of the marketing campaign as amplifying the behavioural change triggered by the context change (residential move). More precisely, the amplifying effect of the campaign should operate through the following two mechanisms:

- Former habitual car users with the intention of switching to PT are confronted with the problem that their knowledge of how to use this transport system is low. Thus a marketing campaign that provides them with all necessary PT knowledge in a convenient and easily understandable way should reduce this central barrier habitual car users are confronted with when trying to follow through on their intention to change their behaviour

- A second way in which the marketing campaign can amplify the change triggered by the move may consist in the delivery of information that supports and enforces former habitual car users' expectation that car use is an unattractive option for daily trips in Munich. Information stressing the monetary and time costs associated with parking or the time loss and stress caused by daily congestion may be effective in strengthening this expectation

7.1.4 Description of the sample

From the Munich municipal office we received the addresses of all 6,200 persons registered as new citizens in the month before the start of the marketing campaign. A random procedure was used to assign 5,000 of these 6,200 addresses to a experimental group and 1,200 to a control group. In the following all 5,000 addresses assigned to the experimental group were included in the dialogue marketing campaign. Because the evaluation budget did not allow all 6,200 new citizens to be interviewed, we drew a random sub-sample of 950 addresses from the 5,000 addresses assigned to the experimental group and also a random sub-sample of 950 addresses from the 1,200 addresses assigned to the control group. These 1,900 addresses form the total gross address sample of the evaluation study, which was conducted from April to June 2006, after the completion of the intervention phase.

To obtain a high participation rate as well as high data quality we decided to collect the evaluation data via personal interviews conducted by trained student interviewers. For this purpose, a letter was sent to all 1,900 addresses announcing the interview in the first step. The letter contained an answer postcard where we asked participants to give us a phone number for fixing the time of the interview. Persons who did not react to the first letter received two additional reminders. Of the 1,900 letters sent out, 17% were undeliverable because of a non-existent or wrong address. About 30% (560) sent back the postcard and agreed to take part in the study. However, despite intensive trials, we succeeded in conducting the interview in only 414 cases. To reduce the self-selection effect potentially associated with the high non-response rate, we decided to try to conduct additional interviews with persons who did not react to our letter and reminders. For this purpose the interviewers went to these addresses directly, rang the bell, and asked for a interview. With this strategy we succeeded in conducting an additional 218 interviews. Later analyses show that persons who were asked for an interview directly at the door more frequently work full-time and use the car for daily trips in Munich more frequently. In total we conducted 632 interviews (302 in the experimental group and 330 in the control group). With respect to the original gross address sample of 1,900 addresses the response rate is 33%; excluding the undeliverable addresses this rises to 40%.

7.2   Results

7.2.1   Independent behavioural effect of the context change

A central hypothesis underlying this research is that the context change created by a residential move itself is the central trigger of changes in habitual car use. The anticipated change in the transport infrastructural conditions at the new residential place should motivate particularly persons moving from villages or small towns to Munich to reduce the number of cars they own and, as a consequence, their access to cars. By voluntarily reducing their access to cars these persons simultaneously interrupt the easy performance of habitual car use and force themselves to use transport alternatives more frequently such as PT in Munich.

To test this hypothesis empirically in the first step participants' old residential places were categorised as follows: villages or small towns (up to 10,000 inhabitants), middle-sized towns (10,001 up to 100,000 inhabitants) and big cities or urban agglomerations (100,001 or more inhabitants). As expected, data analyses indicate strong differences in car ownership, car accessibility as well as car use between participants from these three types of residential area: households moving to Munich from villages or small towns and from medium-sized towns report that they owned a significantly greater number of cars prior to the move than participants who moved to Munich from big cities or urban agglomerations. This difference is reflected in the respective differences in the individual access to a car prior to the move. That the differences in car ownership and car accessibility reflect differences in the transport infrastructure available at the old residential place is indicated by corresponding differences in participants' judgements regarding how easy PT use was at their old place of residence. Whereas participants moving to Munich from a big city or urban agglomeration consider PT use at the old place of residence as quite easy, participants moving from villages or small towns or from medium-sized towns judged PT use at their old place of residence as more difficult. These differences in the available transport infrastructure are probably also the reason why participants from villages or small towns used the car more frequently than PT for daily trips at their old place of residence prior to their move.

Whereas the analyses indicate strong mean differences between participants moving to Munich from different residential areas prior to the move, after the move these differences disappeared. In Munich participants moving from different residential areas no longer showed significant differences in the reported number of cars owned per household or individual access to a car, in the perception of how easy car use is in Munich as well as in their self-reported PT and car use for daily trips in Munich. These results indicate that participants' judgements not only reliably reflect the objective transport infrastructure conditions at their old and new place of residence but also how flexibly they adapted to changes in these conditions. The calculated pre–post move mean changes demonstrate impressively how strongly participants moving to Munich from villages and small towns adapted their car ownership to the new conditions: On average they reduced the number of owned cars from two to one. In the total sample the proportion of participants living in a household without a car increased from 15.4% before the move to 34% after the move. By this decision participants voluntarily 'force' themselves to switch from the car to PT, which is reflected in the decrease in self-reported car use and a corresponding increase in PT use in Munich. Expressed in the standardised effect-size statistic, d (Cohen 1988), the self-reported change in PT use reported by the control group corresponds to an effect-size d statistic of 0.87 and the change in car use to an effect-size d statistic of 0.66. These effect sizes indicate the strong impact of residential context change on daily travel behaviour at the new place of residence.

7.2.2 Results of the process evaluation

The data collected by Omniphon during the intervention phase showed that the information pack could be delivered by mail to 4,526 of the 5,000 households included in the campaign. Of these 4,526 households 1,061 (23%) sent back the service card and requested a total of 10,204 additional brochures. Pocket timetables for specific PT routes were the most frequently requested additional information. Of the 1,061 households using the service card, 350 (33%) requested the offered one-week free PT test ticket. For the 861 households that provide the phone number requested on the service card Omniphon conducted a personal counselling and sales promotion talk via phone, which resulted in 171 requests for order forms for a long-term PT pass (20% of all households called).

During the interview the 302 participants of the experimental group answered questions dealing with their perception, usage and validation of the delivered campaign elements. Of the 302 experimental group members 280 (93%) remembered that they received the information pack. However, only 41% (n = 124) reported that they received it within four weeks after their move to Munich, 30% (n = 319) reported that they received it within two months and 29% (n = 88) received it three months and later after their move. Of the 302 experimental group members 192 (64%) reported that they noticed the additional service card and 149 (49%) reported that they noticed the offered free PT test ticket.

However, the act of noticing campaign elements does not necessarily mean that participants actually use those resources: of the 302 persons in the experimental group 41 (14%) reported that they read the delivered mobility folder intensively, and 117 (39%) reported that they read it partially. Of the 192 persons who noticed the service card, 82 (27% of the overall group) actually used the card to request additional information. Furthermore, 72 (24% of the overall group) reported that they visited websites mentioned in the information parcel for further PT information. Of the 149 persons who noticed the offered free PT test ticket, 55 actually requested the ticket. The delivered city map was the most frequently used campaign element: 199 persons (66% of the overall group) reported that they used the map. Some 80 participants (27%) remembered that they received a phone call from Omniphon. In total, 59 participants (20%) from the experimental group reported that they used none of the campaign material, 19% used at least one campaign element, 32% two elements, 17% three elements, 8% four elements and 3% used all five delivered campaign elements.

7.2.3 Results of the outcome evaluation

Table 7.1 presents the mean differences between the control and experimental groups in the modal split shares of the four travel modes: walking, cycling, PT and car use. The respective modal split shares were calculated on the basis of data obtained from three mobility diaries we asked participants to report for each trip conducted on three different days, detailing where and when the trip started, its purpose (e.g. work, shopping, leisure), the travel mode used (e.g. car, bike, walking or PT), the destination, the time of arrival and the estimated distance.

As can be seen from Table 7.1 data analysis indicates that for the experimental group the share of daily trips in Munich conducted by PT is 7.6 percentage points higher than in the control group. This difference is statistically significant and corresponds to an effect size of $d = 0.23$. The data presented in Table 7.1 also indicate that the experimental group's higher PT use seems to result in less frequent car use (−3.3 percentage points) and in less walking and cycling (−3.5 percentage points) than the control group. However, the design power is not high enough to decide whether the observed differences in car use, walking and cycling represents systematic effects of the campaign or simply random fluctuation.

The results of t-tests indicate for the experimental group a significantly higher degree of PT-related knowledge (mean of experimental group = 3.47 compared with mean of control group = 3.21, $p < 0.05$) as well as a significantly lower expectation that car use in Munich is easy ($M = -0.56$ vs. $M = -0.28$, $p < 0.05$). Further path analyses show that the behavioural effect of the marketing cam-

TABLE 7.1   Effect of the dialogue marketing campaign on movers' travel mode choice for daily trips in Munich: percentage modal split

Travel mode	Experimental group N = 298		Control group N = 324		Statistical test of mean differences		
	M	SD	M	SD	Difference	t	p
Walking	22.3	0.26	23.5	0.26	−1.2	−0.53	0.30
Cycling	7.1	0.19	9.4	0.22	−2.3	−1.43	0.08
Public transport	41.3	0.36	33.7	0.33	+7.6	+2.78	< 0.01
Car	27.0	0.34	30.3	0.36	−3.3	−1.18	0.12

M = mean; SD = standard deviation; p relates to the results of one-sided t-tests

Note: the modal split shares are calculated on the basis of the data obtained from three mobility diaries. The PT category also includes trips where PT use was combined with other means. The car category includes trips conducted as driver as well as passenger. The lower sample size (N = 622) results from the fact that only persons who reported at least one trip in the mobility diaries are included in the analysis. Because the table does not report the share of trips conducted by means categorised by the respondents as 'miscellaneous', the reported modal split shares do not sum to 100%.

paign is completely mediated by its direct positive effect on PT knowledge ($\beta = 0.11$) and its direct negative effect on the perceived convenience of car use in Munich ($\beta = -0.08$).

7.2.4 Learning experiences

The evaluation of the marketing campaign indicates that combining the context change of residential relocation with a marketing campaign is an effective strategy to change habitual car use. In the experimental group the PT modal split share is 7.6 percentage points higher than in the control group. Because of the randomised control trial design this difference can be causally attributed to the effect of the marketing campaign. The observed mean difference corresponds to an effect size of 0.23 which indicates a small effect. However, in the transport domain where most information-oriented interventions have a zero effect, this small effect is of great practical significance. The evaluation results also indicate that the marketing campaign had a specific behavioural impact. The main change in travel behaviour consists in movers' increased use of PT for daily trips, which seems to result half from less car use and half from less walking and cycling. Thus from an environmental policy viewpoint a negative side-effect of the marketing campaign is that it seems to motivate not only former car user to use PT more frequently but also persons who formally walked and cycled. The significance of the present study consists not only in the fact that because of the randomised control trial the estimated treatment effect size has a high internal validity but that the results also have a high external validity: the study results are based on a random sample of movers, personal interviews were used as a data-collection method and considerable labour was invested in reducing potential self-selection processes. Furthermore, the financial budget and collaboration with a marketing company allowed a high degree of professionalism in the development, production and delivery of the campaign, which is frequently a weakness of academically conducted intervention studies. To summarise, the present evaluation provides a reliable estimate of the average behavioural effect one can expect from a professionally conducted marketing campaign involving dialogues with movers to German urban agglomeration such as Munich.

Concerning the mechanisms mediating the impact of the residential relocation on movers' travel behaviour the data analyses provide strong evidence that the anticipatory reduction of car ownership plays a central role. In particular, persons moving from rural areas to Munich reported a very high degree of car ownership at their old place of residence. Prior to the move in these households the average number of cars corresponded to the average number of persons living in a household (two in each case) or, in other words, on average each household member owned a car. Probably the high number of cars reflects the car-oriented transport infrastructure in rural areas. The expectation that they will have access to a high-quality PT service in Munich in a situation where car use will become less attractive obviously motivates particularly persons from rural areas to reduce the car number to one per household. As a consequence individual access to a car also decreases, which 'forces' participants to use PT more frequently. The results also confirm that the independent additional behavioural effect of the marketing campaign is mediated by its positive direct impact on PT knowledge as well as its direct negative impact on the perception of how easy car use is in Munich.

What are the practical implications of these results? For me, personally, the most impressive result consists in the flexibility with which people voluntarily adapt their travel behaviour to changes in objective infrastructural conditions associated with their move to Munich. Under the new infrastructural conditions the majority of former car users decided to use PT more frequently than the car for daily trips. In Munich in the control group as well the PT modal split share is higher than the car modal split share. Even more impressive is the finding that after the move a considerable number of households clearly decided to completely give up car ownership: After the move the proportion of participants living in households without a car increased from 15.4% to 34%. This result is in sharp contrast to the frequent public as well as academic view of car ownership and car use as a deep-rooted cultural matter, which would therefore of course to a large extent be resistant to external influences. Instead, the present results indicate that people quickly change their car ownership as well as their habitual car use if they have the expectation that the outcome an alternative transport option affords is more desirable than those offered by car use. To summarise, the present results indicate that the critical point for 'breaking' a car use habit is to create conditions that make other transport alternatives more attractive and/or car use less attractive. Under such conditions a change away from habitual car use seems to be less difficult than frequently assumed in the literature. The impact on behaviour of context changes such as a residential move seem to rely mainly on their function as 'windows of opportunity'. Context changes provide people with a reason and/or incentive to consciously re-evaluate whether their old travel habits will deliver the best outcomes under the new contextual conditions or whether the use of other transport options will produce more desirable outcomes.

However, the behavioural consequences of the conscious re-evaluation caused by the context change depend to a large extent on the objective infrastructural conditions provided by the new context. If people move from an urban agglomeration to a rural area this context change will probably result in 'breaking' their former PT use habit and an increase in car ownership and car use. This implies also that the behavioural effectiveness of campaigns aiming to motivate people to use environmentally friendly transportation modes more frequently will depend on objective conditions. The behavioural effect of campaigns such as that evaluated in the present study hold true only for urban agglomerations such as Munich. In rural areas with low PT service quality a similar marketing campaign will probably have no effect.

However, under the right conditions a professionally conducted downstream-plus-context-change intervention can obviously make a substantive difference. From the present results one can derive clear recommendations as to which mechanisms such an intervention should focus on: it should try to deliver to movers, as soon as possible and in a way as convenient and as understandable as possible, (1) the knowledge necessary to use the PT system and (2) information and arguments supporting and amplifying movers' expectations that at the new residential place car use is an unattractive and difficult-to-use alternative. Future studies systematically analysing the type of information or arguments and through which communication channels best fit the needs of former car users would make a valuable contribution to increasing the effectiveness of such campaigns.

7.3 Potential for diffusion and scaling up

From my point of view the downstream-plus-context-change strategy has great potential for diffusion. In Germany alone about four million people move each year (Statistisches Bundesamt 2001). Furthermore, in principle, the downstream-plus-context-change strategy could be implemented at many significant life-stage changes that people experience naturally during the course of their lives. Such changes occur with some regularity across the life-span and often coincide with people's movement into another life-phase, such as adolescents leaving their parents' home, couples starting a family and older people entering retirement.

References

Aarts, H., B. Verplanken and A. Knippenberg (1998) 'Predicting Behaviour from Actions in the Past: Repeated Decision-making or a Matter of Habit?', *Journal of Applied Social Psychology* 28: 1,355-74.

Bamberg, S. (2006) 'Is a Residential Relocation a Good Opportunity to Change People's Travel Behaviour? Results From a Theory-Driven Intervention Study', *Environment and Behaviour* 38: 820-40.

Brög, W., E. Erl and N. Mense (2003) 'Individualised Marketing Changing Travel Behaviour for a Better Environment', paper presented at the TRIP research conference: *The Economic and Environmental Consequences of Regulating Traffic*, Hillerød, 2–3 February 2003.

Bühl, A. (2002) 'Informationen zum ÖPNV bei Zuzug und Umzug: Vom Projekt zum festen Angebot' (brochure; Heidelberg, Germany: Stadt Heidelberg, Heidelberger Straßen- und Bergbahn AG).

Cohen, J. (1988) *Statistical Power Analysis for the Behavioural Sciences* (Hillsdale, NJ: Lawrence Erlbaum, 2nd edn).

Gärling, T., and K.W. Axhausen (2003) 'Introduction: Habitual Travel Choice', *Transportation* 30: 1-11.

Loose, W. (2004) 'ÖPNV-Begrüßungspaket und Schnupperticket für Neubürger: Bericht zur Evaluation der Maßnahme zum ÖPNV-Direktmarketing' (Working Paper 2004-033-de; Freiburg: Öko-Institut EV).

Statistisches Bundesamt (2001) *Statistisches Jahrbuch 2001 für die Bundesrepublik Deutschland* (Wiesbaden, Germany: Statistisches Bundesamt).

Thøgersen, J. (2006) 'Understanding Repetitive Travel Mode Choices in a Stable Context: A Panel Study Approach', *Transportation Research Part A: Policy and Practice* 40: 621-38.

Verplanken, B., and H. Aarts (1999) 'Habit, Attitude, and Planned Behaviour: Is Habit an Empty Construct or an Interesting Case of Goal-Directed Automaticity?', *European Review of Social Psychology* 10: 101-34.

—— and W. Wood (2006) 'Changing and Breaking Habits', *Journal of Public Policy and Marketing* 25: 90-103.

8
The London congestion charge scheme

An Vercalsteren and Theo Geerken

Flemish Institute for Technological Research (VITO), Belgium

Congestion is a classic example of the overuse of a common resource to which there is free access. The fact that additional road users slow down other drivers but do not perceive this as a cost leads to overuse of the road network. This initiated the idea of road pricing, which had already been discussed in Britain in the 1960s, with the booming of the car fleet. Congestion charging is one example of road pricing.

The principal objective of congestion charging is to reduce traffic congestion in and around the charging zone by reducing the amount of traffic within that zone. A congestion charge scheme has been introduced in several cities around the world, but the most well-known European example is the one in London, UK.

The basic principle of the London congestion charge is that consumers should pay for the costs they impose as an incentive to use the road network more efficiently. This reflects also the principle that one should pay more for a scarce resource, which is in this case the available road. The system in London was first introduced by the then Mayor of London, Ken Livingstone (a top-down decision). However, the final decision to go ahead was preceded by a long research and consultation period, starting in 1995. Before the congestion charge was introduced, London suffered from the worst traffic congestion in the UK. In Central

London average traffic speeds decreased below 10 miles per hour (mph). Ken Livingstone promised (in his mayoral election manifesto) to consult on a congestion charge scheme for Central London. On 17 February 2003 the Central London Congestion Charging Scheme was introduced and in February 2007 was extended to the west of London.

8.1 Case description

8.1.1 Overview

The congestion charge scheme was initiated to counter the congestion problems Central London had been dealing with since the 1990s. As already stated above, the then Mayor of London, Ken Livingstone, considered it his highest priority to resolve London's transport problems, among which was the reduction of traffic congestion. His goal was to create a world-class transport system that enhances business efficiency, supports greater economic prosperity and improves the quality of life for every resident and visitor to London. The congestion charge scheme is thus only one aspect of a wider transport strategy that focuses not only on congestion problems but also on radically improving public transport, increasing the capacity of London's transport system, improving journey time reliability for car users and so on. The specific goal of the congestion charge scheme is to encourage people to think again about using their vehicles in Central London and to choose other forms of transport if possible.

In February 2003 the congestion charge scheme was finally introduced through the Greater London Congestion Charging 2001 Scheme Order (legal framework).[1] The introduction of the congestion charge scheme in London was a top-down decision, enforced by the London local government, but nevertheless efforts were made to consult public opinion on the issue as much as possible.

The congestion charge in London is a fixed daily charge for driving or parking a vehicle on public roads within the congestion charging zone. Payment of the daily charge allows one to drive around, leave and re-enter the charging zone as many times as required in one day. The scheme initially covered 22 km² in Central London and operated only on weekdays from 7.00 am to 6.00 pm (excluding holidays). The charging area is indicated by roadside signs and by symbols painted on the road. The scheme is enforced with use of cameras in and around the charging zone. Drivers entering the charging zone have their vehicle num-

---

1 For more on the history and further details on the London congestion charge, visit its website, at www.cclondon.com, accessed 18 March 2009.

ber plate read by the cameras, using automatic number plate recognition (ANPR) technology. The vehicle registration number is then stored in a central database. When drivers pay the charge, they register via their individual vehicle registration number. Payment can be made by post, telephone, the internet, SMS, self-service machines, retail outlets and some petrol stations. Specific vehicle categories are exempt—taxis, minicabs, buses and motorcycles as well as certain alternative-fuel vehicles. Other 'vehicle categories' can register for discounts: that is, residents in the charging zone (90% discount) and disabled people (100% discount).

Looking at the success criteria in relation to the introduction of a congestion charge in London, it shows that Central London is particularly suitable for congestion pricing because of its limited road capacity (the street network in the core area has hardly expanded since the Middle Ages) and heavy travel demand resulting in severe congestion. London also has relatively good travel alternatives, including walking, taxi, bus and subway (London Underground) services. Furthermore, it was decided that all the revenue generated would be invested in transport in London for at least ten years. The congestion charge scheme is accompanied by a wide range of measures designed to make public transport easier, cheaper, faster and more reliable, which is an important aspect of the success of the charging scheme.

Another aspect that influenced the feasibility and success of congestion charging in London was the technology used to register the cars that enter the zone (ANPR). The success of the system also depends on the efficiency and failure rate of this technology. In the beginning of congestion charging, some problems occurred with, on the one hand, the technology to register the cars and, on the other hand, the users of the system, who had no experience with the payment facilities. Both problems were solved within a few months of the introduction of the charge.

The congestion charge scheme is closely monitored and, if appropriate, variations are proposed to the scheme to make adjustments and improvements to it or to extend it (as in February 2007). As well as the follow-up of the legal and operational aspects, a comprehensive impact monitoring programme is in operation. This results in annual reports that describe the impacts of the congestion charge. The reports also cover the key traffic, transport and operational outcomes for the previous year and the business, social, economic and environmental impacts of the scheme.

8.1.2 Case context: landscape and regime

At the time the first in-depth research was begun to analyse the feasibility of congestion charge in London the city suffered from the worst traffic congestion in the UK and even among the worst in Europe. Around 2000, almost 1.1 million people entered Central London during the morning peak hours, of whom approximately 13% used public transport. In Central London average traffic speeds decreased below 20 km h^{-1} between 1998 and 2000. It was calculated that drivers in Central London spent 50% of their travel time in queues. The delays harmed the city's economy as the created huge losses in terms of time and money. It has been estimated that London lost between £2 million and £4 million every week in terms of lost time caused by congestion. At that time there was a general consensus that something needed to be done to tackle the problem.

In this context the following factors can be identified: infrastructure, technology and behaviour. The infrastructure refers to the road network, for which the government is responsible (construction, maintenance, etc.). The vehicles that are used are the responsibility of the automotive industry (producers), in terms of technology used. A third factor that can be distinguished relates to the consumers as users of the vehicles and the road network. In particular, factors related to infrastructure and behaviour are influenced by congestion charging. The government created a framework that obliges people to pay for the use of the road network. By doing so consumers are prompted to change their behaviour, as before the charge people were free to drive through Central London whereas after the introduction of the charge they had to pay for using the road network in that area.

8.1.3 Actors and their roles and perspectives

As the congestion charge in London was really pushed forward by one man, assisted by a whole group of people (politicians, researchers, etc.), the primary actor in this case is the Mayor of London, Ken Livingstone. He recognised the need to take action regarding London's traffic jams and took the responsibility (and risk) to introduce congestion charging as an efficient system to tackle the traffic problems in Central London.

Secondary actors in this regard are the key stakeholders such as local councils, businesses and road-user representatives that were consulted during the preceding consultation and research phase. Their comments on the initial proposal were taken into account for the final document that discussed the congestion charge in London. It should be noted that during the preparation many actors were much more critical than after the implementation of the congestion charge scheme. This is more thoroughly discussed below.

8.1.4 Case history and development

Before actually introducing the congestion charge in London many years of research and public consultation passed. In 1995 the Government Office for London published the results of the London Congestion Research Programme. This report examined a range of technical options and projected substantial decongestion benefits of such a scheme operating in London. In 1999 the power and responsibility to manage the city's transport system and to raise taxes to fund transport improvements were given to the Mayor by law. This allowed the Mayor to introduce congestion charging in London. To inform mayoral candidates about the implications of the different charging options, an independent group was assigned to report on this (the Review Of Charging Options for London [ROCOL] group). Ken Livingstone announced during his election that he wanted to take forward the ROCOL proposals with regard to a congestion charging scheme for Central London. This included the decision to introduce congestion charging in Central London and to use the revenue for funding improvements to public transport. After his election Ken Livingstone proceeded with the congestion charge plan, but it was only after an extensive public consultation phase that he finally decided to proceed with congestion charging as the best way forward to reduce traffic congestion in Central London. An important decision related to the scheme was to reinvest all the revenue generated by the congestion charge in transport in London for at least ten years. A large amount of money was made available to implement traffic management measures to complement the scheme and to minimise any adverse effects.

It was expected that congestion charging would result in substantial decreases in 'road' traffic. Modelling predicted that inside the charging zone:

- Traffic would be reduced by 10–15% (expressed in vehicle kilometres)
- Queues would be reduced by 20–30% (expressed in vehicle delays)
- Traffic speeds would be increased by 10–15%

Outside the charging zone, both positive and negative effects were expected:

- Traffic on orbital routes (such as the inner ring road) might increase by up to 5%
- Traffic on radial routes would be reduced by 5–10%
- An overall reduction in traffic of 1–2% would be accomplished

Although some areas outside the central zone may experience a small increase in traffic, congestion charging was expected to reduce the overall levels of congestion both inside and outside the charging zone. Overall, journey times and deliveries would be much more reliable for those people making essential journeys within the charging zone. It was expected that drivers would save 2–3 million hours within the zone each year.

In a first consultation phase, key stakeholders such as local councils, businesses and road-user representatives were involved. Based on their comments a draft transport strategy was elaborated. During a public consultation, people were given the opportunity to comment on the draft transport strategy, including the proposed Central London congestion charge scheme. The consultation phase concluded that the majority of key stakeholders supported the scheme and, as a result, the final transport strategy was published in 2001 (Livingstone 2001). Based on further public consultation, modifications were introduced and in 2002 the legal framework was finished to proceed with congestion charging. During this process the Mayor was supported by Transport for London (TfL), the organisation that manages the congestion charge scheme. However, numerous groups were largely opposed to the scheme. Even during the election phase, the plan to introduce a congestion charge in London was criticised by various interest groups (politicians, motorist groups and labour organisations). Another mayoral candidate even promised to end the congestion pricing programme if elected (Litman 2006). Also, many newspapers were sceptical about or were opposed to the programme. One issue of concern was that nearby roads would become congested as a result of diverted traffic, but the reality has been that this effect appears to be very small. In addition, the system of tracking vehicles was considered to be an invasion of privacy.

However, since the introduction of the scheme in 2003 the congestion pricing programme has been generally accepted by the public and interest groups, including some of the initial opponents such as automobile clubs. Within one month of implementation residents in other areas of London requested to be included, and the political arena ended its opposition to the charge. This acceptance of the scheme was corroborated in the re-election of Ken Livingstone, which was largely a result of the success of the congestion charge programme and his plans to expand the zone (Litman 2006). Recently, with the election of the new Mayor of London Boris Johnson, the situation has changed somewhat. He promised in his election programme to reduce the charging zone; however, at present this is yet to be enforced.

8.2 Results

8.2.1 Main results

The organisation that manages the scheme, TfL, planned a comprehensive impact monitoring programme. A report is published annually that discusses the impacts of the congestion charge in London and compares these actual impacts with the expected impacts of the programme.

The most recent publications (TfL 2006; TfL 2008) discuss the results of the congestion charge after three to five years of implementation. General results are summarised below:

- Traffic patterns in and around the charging area remained stable over the three years. Changes to the scheme in July 2005 were responsible for only small net reductions in traffic volumes. Overall, traffic patterns are broadly the same since the implementation of the scheme

- Reductions in congestion inside the charging zone averaged 26% over the first three years but have since been eroded (due to a reduced effective road network capacity)

- Traffic conditions inside and outside the charging zone were influenced by the reallocation of network capacity to meet other policy objectives, such as improved pedestrian safety and amenity. The effect of the charging scheme therefore needs to be assessed in this context

- Public transport continues to successfully accommodate displaced car users, and bus services continue to benefit from improved reliability

- Economic trend data demonstrate that there are no significant net impacts from the scheme on the business performance of the Central London economy

- Gains in terms of reduced road traffic accidents and emission of key traffic pollutants in and around the charging zone are apparent, alongside favourable 'background' trends in both of these indicators

- Adjustments on road network capacity have resulted in improved safety and amenity and increased priority for buses, taxis and cyclists. In other words, the motor-vehicle-moving capacity of the network has been adjusted in favour of the people-moving capacity of the network

- The congestion charge scheme has tended to accentuate pre-existing positive trends and reverse negative trends in traffic patterns, while having a broadly neutral impact on the London economy and social activities

8.2.2 Change in sustainability performance

8.2.2.1 Environmental improvement

Congestion, defined as the excess delay (expressed as minutes per kilometre), decreased in the charging zone by 25–30% compared with pre-charging conditions. Congestion also decreased slightly on both the boundary road to the charging zone and the main radial routes because of improved traffic management arrangements, but it is now slowly increasing again. However, this increasing congestion reflects a longer-term trend, as the same is observed on all main inner-London roads.

It was expected that congestion charging would lead to increased travel by public transport, as former car occupants switched to alternative modes of transport. To anticipate this increased demand substantial enhancements to the public transport service were put in place. Congestion charging indeed has led to a substantial increase in the number of people entering Central London by bus during charging hours (37% in 2003 compared with the 2002 level, with an even greater increase in 2004). Some 50% of this increase is assessed as being primarily the result of the introduction of the congestion charge. The remainder reflects a background trend of growth in bus patronage. Thanks to enhancements to the public transport network, this increased passenger demand did not cause overpopulation of public transport (e.g. buses) in the area. Also, the reliability of public transport improved, which is an important precondition for the success of the congestion charge effect.

Based on the observation of a 15% reduction in road traffic and a 30% reduction in congestion, an initial assessment of the impact of the scheme on key road traffic emissions has been performed by the authorised organisation. This assessment has led to the conclusion that, on major roads within the charging zone, total primary emissions of nitrogen oxides NO_x and particulates (PM10) decreased by 16%; 12% of this is attributed to traffic changes, the remainder to background changes such as improved vehicle technology and a renewal of the fleet. Most important for this reduction is the reduced congestion in the area. On the boundary roads (e.g. inner ring road) no significant reduction in emissions was noticed. The assessment also estimated that the congestion charging led to a reduction of up to 20% in both fossil fuel use and CO_2 emissions. Sample surveys of ambient noise in and around the charging zone suggest no detectible impact from congestion charging.

8.2.2.2 Social improvements

With regard to traffic patterns, monitoring shows that traffic adjusted rapidly to the introduction of the scheme; only few operational traffic problems occurred. One of the key results is that traffic circulating within the charging zone reduced by 15% during charging hours (monitored as vehicle-kilometres driven) compared to pre-charging levels. Traffic entering the charging zone during charging hours decreased by 18%. Both results approach the most optimistic expectations of the organisation responsible for the implementation and follow-up of the congestion charging scheme. As expected, the traffic just outside the charging zone increased (with the inner ring road as the boundary of the charging zone); however, this increase was smaller than expected and did not lead to operational problems. Analysis of longer-term traffic trends in the rest of London points to overall background reductions in traffic levels dating from the late 1990s. In any case, monitoring showed no evidence of adverse traffic impacts on roads surrounding the charging zone.

The introduction of the scheme also resulted in changes in travel behaviour, as a response to the scheme. The biggest change prompted by congestion charging can be noticed in the transfer of car users to another mode of transport: 60–70% of all former car movements have transferred to another mode of transport. The majority of these switched from using the car to the bus, Underground or over-ground train. A smaller group transferred to walking, cycling, motorcycling or taxi. An important remark in this context is that this change in travel behaviour occurs for those that do not live in the charging zone. People living in the charging zone have not radically changed their travel behaviour, which may be explained by the fact that they receive a 90% discount on the congestion charge fee.

The social impacts of the scheme are monitored by examining to what extent people felt they are affected by the scheme and associated change. A distinction must be made between people living in the charging zone and those living outside the charging zone but regularly travelling to Central London for work or leisure. People living inside the charging zone are positive about the change in their local area, particularly the reduction in congestion. Also, people visiting the charging area specifically acknowledge the general amenity of the area, air quality, noise, traffic levels and public transport provision.

8.2.2.3 Economic improvements

At the time of the introduction of congestion charging, the London economy was experiencing a big slowdown. It has now recovered from that slowdown. Extensive research showed that congestion charging had a broadly neutral impact on overall business performance in the charging zone. Measurement of business performance in terms of variables such as employment, numbers of businesses, turnover and profitability failed to find any evidence of an effect from the scheme. It can be concluded that congestion charging had a neutral impact on the economy of Central London and that any impacts on individual business sectors, including retailing, are small.

It is fair to conclude that the congestion charge scheme in London led to an improved living environment for inner-city residents and for commuters as a result of a reduction in traffic jams and congestion. Strongly related to the implementation of the congestion charging are the improvements with regard to public transport. Both the congestion charge and the improved public transport system led to a change in travel behaviour by London's inhabitants and commuters, which in turn led to a significant reduction in emissions (NO_x, $PM10$, CO_2) in the charging zone.

8.2.3 Learning experiences

The London case confirms that systems such as congestion charging are especially successful when consumers are experiencing problems with the current situation. The theory 'no pain, no change' applies to the case of London congestion charging. The traffic problems were so great that most people (including the car drivers in the area) agreed that something had to be done. This is one of the reasons why the congestion charge in London experienced no great opposition and is largely accepted by all stakeholders.

An important precondition for the success of such a scheme is the need to offer good alternatives to car transport. In London the bus network was largely improved and extended before the introduction of the scheme, and public transport in general has improved since the introduction of the congestion charge.

It is important that the users of the system—the people that pay the charge—are well informed about what happens with the money that is charged. In this regard the fact that the charges for the London case are reinvested for the improvement of transport in general in London leads to 'social support' for the scheme. It is not considered as 'just another tax to feed the treasury'.

There is, of course, still potential for improvement to the scheme. One often-cited point of criticism is that the congestion charge in London prices entrance rather than use. Indeed, the charge is not based on the number of miles a vehicle is driven within the charging area, nor is it time-variable, which means the fee is not higher during the most congested periods. The government accepts this criticism but argues that the current system was chosen because it could be implemented in a relatively short time and is easy to understand. A more sophisticated system that allows variable fees is planned for the future. The scheme is able to be fine-tuned as it operates, meaning it has flexibility in terms of pricing and geographical reach. This flexibility is already evident in increases in the fee and an extension of the charging area.

The high overhead cost of the system is another issue of criticism. A substantial part of the revenue is used to pay programme expenses. Critics argue that there are more cost-effective ways to collect money. However, as a congestion reduction strategy and a way to improve public transport (with a focus on bus transport) it has proven to be an effective and cost-efficient investment.

8.3 Potential for diffusion and scaling up

One of the major obstacles to the introduction of congestion charging in other cities is the political resistance, because of the expected resistance from residents (and thus voters). Therefore, the London congestion charge is considered an important test of the political feasibility of congestion pricing in major cities. London's experience shows that such a system is technically feasible and effective. Moreover, it is possible to overcome the political and institutional resistance to such a system if there is a lack of acceptable alternatives. The congestion charge experience in London indicates that private automobile travel is more price-sensitive than was widely believed. However, better pricing systems are needed to optimise the incentive, with prices that depend on the type of vehicle, the time and the distance travelled in the charging zone. This is technically feasible; however, a fixed charge is more easy to implement during the startup phase. Experiences in London have also demonstrated that the implementation of such a system is not easy and requires a good combination of travel, infrastructure and political conditions.

When residents are sufficiently frustrated with traffic problems in their city and when political conditions are amenable to innovative solutions, other cities can consider implementing congestion pricing. As soon as consumers (car drivers) experience substantial problems because of traffic overload, an important incentive for change exists.

In London in 2007 the congestion charge was 'scaled up', with the extension of the charging zone to the west. A specific adjustment in this regard has been the exemption of a number of routes from the scheme to enable vehicles to cross the zone during charging hours without paying.

8.4 Overall conclusions

Of the different methods authorities can impose to reduce traffic levels towards a more optimal level, congestion charging is favoured over other methods such as traffic bans (e.g. Athens) because it ensures that those drivers who value their journey least will forgo it. This way drivers set to gain the lowest benefit from their journey alter their behaviour. Another benefit from congestion charging is that it raises revenue, which ideally should be used to improve public transport alternatives and the general transport infrastructure.

The London case shows that when all incentives are in place—political willingness, technological feasibility and consumers experiencing nuisance because of the traffic conditions—the introduction of a congestion charging system has a large chance of success. In this case the government (led by the Mayor of London) was willing to do something drastic that would perhaps be unpopular in order to tackle traffic jams in Central London. The technology to enable a congestion charge system had already been developed and was on the market and, furthermore, people driving in Central London were experiencing substantial problems with congestion, such as time delays. All these factors positively influenced the success of the London congestion charge.

In conclusion, this case shows that the social (time saving) and environmental (reduction in emissions) advantages of congestion charging are evident, with no noticeable economic drawbacks for business performance. Evidently, all remaining drivers benefited from time savings. Furthermore, the congestion charge resulted in a change in mainstream consumer behaviour (which can be noticed in the high percentage of car users transferring to another mode of transport) and a changed travel pattern into Central London.

References

Livingstone, K. (2001) *The Mayor's Transport Strategy* (London: Greater London Authority).

TfL (Transport for London) (2006) *Central London Congestion Charging Impacts Monitoring: Fourth Annual Report* (London: TfL).

—— (2008) *Central London Congestion Charging Impacts Monitoring: Sixth Annual Report* (London: TfL).

Further reading

Blow, L., A. Leicester and Z. Smith (2003) *London's Congestion Charge: Briefing Note 31* (London: Institute for Fiscal Studies)

Holdsworth M. (2004) *Sixteen Pain-Free Ways to Help Save the Planet* (London: National Consumer Council).

Litman, T. (2006) *London Congestion Pricing: Implications for Other Cities* (Victoria, Canada: Victoria Transport Policy Institute).

Liu, E., J. Wu and J. Lee (2006) *Monitoring of Mass Transit Systems* (Hong Kong: Research and Library Services Division, Legislative Council Secretariat).

T&E (European Federation for Transport and Environment) (2003) *Congestion Pricing in London: A European Perspective* (Brussels: T&E).

TfL (Transport for London) (2005) *Central London Congestion Charging Impacts Monitoring: Third Annual Report* (London: TfL).

9
Consumer-oriented strategies for car purchases

An analysis of environmental information tools and taxation schemes in The Netherlands

Jorrit Nijhuis and Sander van den Burg

Wageningen University, The Netherlands

Research on environmental policy points to a change in policy instruments being used, emphasising that economic instruments, voluntary agreements and the provision of environmental information, most commonly through labels, are becoming more important. These changes point to new forms of governance that seek to enrol the consumer in the environmental reform of production and consumption chains. As labelling makes more information available to consumers at the crucial places where the consumption end meets the production end of the chain, consumers can play a greater role in co-governing environmental performance through their consumption. Therefore, these consumer strategies have been noted to influence both the consumption and the production part of the chain (Van den Burg 2006; Mol 2008).

The empirical focus of this chapter is on different environmental information tools, most notably the European Union's Labelling Directive (EC 1999) and the supporting taxation schemes that were developed in The Netherlands from 2001 onwards as new consumer-oriented strategies. In this case we combine a policy analysis of these consumer strategies with a practice-oriented approach on the purchasing of new cars. This way, on the one hand, insight is gained into the processes underlying the emergence of these new governance arrangements; on the other hand, we can compare how the expectations of these institutional actors have worked out at the 'micro level' in the showroom. The Dutch case is ideal, for two reasons. First, the Dutch energy-efficiency label is believed to approach the ideal model for car labels (Energieverwertungsagentur 1999). Second, the label (introduced in January 2001) was accompanied by a subsidy programme in 2002. This was abolished a year later but reintroduced in 2006. The accompanying debate concerning these, what some call, inconsistencies can illustrate different views on the role consumers can play in the greening of production and consumption chains.

We will describe the following aspects: first, we portray the social practice of car purchasing and the relevant trends influencing this practice; second, we describe the implementation and developments of the European fuel-efficiency label (as the major information tool); third, based on research conducted in collaboration with Toyota Netherlands, we discuss how different actors assess the environmental information tools and tax schemes that aim to influence consumer car purchase decisions. This assessment is matched with a sustainability impact assessment of the energy-efficiency label.

9.1 Case description

9.1.1 Overview

In Section 9.1.3 the specific targets and organisational structures of the different environmental tools are discussed. Here, we limit ourselves by stating that consumer-oriented strategies in the purchase of new cars have the objective of providing potential consumers with environmental information in order to influence the purchase decision. An additional aim is to stimulate market demand for environmentally friendly cars.

9.1.2 Case context: landscape and regime factors

9.1.2.1 Trends in the automotive sector

An influential landscape factor is the current position of the automotive sector. This sector is characterised by an enormously competitive market in which an increasingly reduced number of regime players operate. This competitiveness is strengthened by a production process that requires huge investments leading to equally high break-even points (Orsato and Wells 2007; Orsato and Clegg 2005; Nieuwenhuis and Wells 1997). The stress on these players is increasingly tight because of environmental regulations in Europe and the USA (e.g. CAFE [Corporate Average Fuel Economy] standards and Auto Oil Programmes [Greene 1998]). However, these regulations did drive an important change in the attitude of car manufacturers; the vast majority of which have adopted a proactive approach in order to decrease the environmental effects of car manufacturing and car use.

A second trend is the change in information provision. The coming of the 'information age' had an enormous influence on the purchasing process of complex products, including car purchasing. Traditionally, automotive dealers were seen as the dominant source of information, resulting in a situation of consumer–salesperson interfaces in which the salesperson 'led' the customer through the buying process (Reed *et al.* 2004). Market research conducted in Germany by TNS Emnid (2004) showed a number of interesting developments in the automotive sector. The practice of information seeking has shifted in such a way that the majority of people purchasing a car make use of the internet as a source of information, making the internet one of the most dominant information sources.

Interestingly enough, another related development that can be witnessed is the decrease in customer ties, meaning that formerly fixed customer–supplier relations have become increasingly fluid. Though important brand differences remain, in general, emotional attachment to a specific brand has lessened as a consequence of increased similarity and decreased quality differences in automobiles. The result is that in the past decade a strongly increased consumer empowerment has taken place. Car vending site Edmunds has summarised this development with its slogan: 'negotiate like a pro'.[1] Not only have car salespeople noticed that consumers enter the showroom armed with background information about the automotive sector, but also the process itself has also changed; instead of visiting ten different showrooms, most consumers make a pre-selection of approximately three car types that they investigate intensively. As a consequence, the role of the salesperson likewise has shifted from leading to guiding, and from salesperson to advisor.

Furthermore, there is a general trend in consumption towards more comfort and convenience. This trend, together with higher safety requirements, has led to an increased demand in size and luxury levels of cars (Van den Brink and Van Wee 2001). As Shove (2003) indicates, what starts out as an extra capacity or

---

1 An important note here is that there might be a significant difference between second-hand car purchasers and new car purchasers. Furthermore, Lambert-Pandraud *et al.* (2005) have pointed out that older consumers, who constitute an important market segment, repurchase a brand more frequently when they buy a new car.

FIGURE 9.1 Developments in average fuel consumption and car weight

Source: European Centre for Mobility Documentation (ECMD)

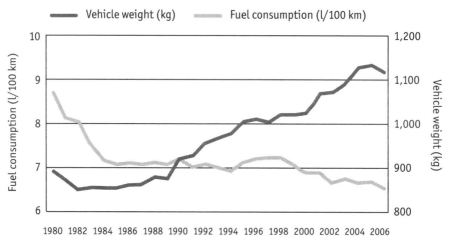

Average car fuel consumption and average car weight
of the top 50 best-selling petrol cars

luxury can soon become normality, thus shifting consumer preferences and expectancies for automobile characteristics. As a consequence, the price of an average new car in The Netherlands has risen from €3,389 in 1970 to €25,742 for petrol cars and €27,396 for diesel cars;[2] more importantly, the fuel consumption has not seen any substantial decrease in the past 25 years (see Fig. 9.1). Recently, fuel consumption has decreased more rapidly; nevertheless, the average decrease since 2001 is still only 1% a year (PBL 2009).

9.1.2.2 Consumers' new car purchasing process

In economics and marketing literature the purchase of a car is defined as a form of 'complex buying behaviour' (Reed *et al.* 2004).[3] Given that the car is a high-

---

2 This figure represents the catalogue price as it is paid by consumers. Ignoring environmental subsidies, it is made up of the following three components: the price of the vehicle (net catalogue price), 66%; the private motor vehicle tax, 21%; and the regular VAT, 13%.

3 Complex buying behaviour means that consumers are highly involved in the purchase; the product itself is expensive, is bought infrequently, is perceived to be risky and is highly self-expressive.

involvement product, the car-buying process is seen as a high-involvement process, leading to active search and use of information, deliberate evaluation of alternatives and a careful choice. More specifically, the consumer information search itself usually includes both 'internal search' (retrieval of information based on previous searches and personal experiences) and 'external search' (accessing of different types of information sources) (Klein and Ford 2003). Furthermore, research has highlighted that the car purchase can be seen as a two-stage process; in the first stage the vehicle class is decided on, based on costs and car capabilities, whereas in the second stage consumers undertake a more profound review of vehicles (Lane 2005; Teisl *et al.* 2007).

When we look at stated preferences we can observe that environmental factors currently do not seem to play a major role in consumer car choices (see the bold items in Table 9.1).

So, even though consumers mention sustainability issues as a major consumer concern (see NIDO 2002), the infamous attitude–action gap reveals that consumers' concern for environmental impact does not often translate into behavioural change (Lane 2005). Furthermore, even though fuel consumption is mentioned as an important factor, for most car buyers little effort is expended in comparisons of fuel consumption during the decision-making process (Boardman *et al.* 2000; Lane 2005).

One conclusion could be that people tend to be more concerned about status value and less about environmental performance then people would like to admit to themselves (Johansson-Stenman and Martinsson 2006). This would fit well into the often-heard claim made by policy-makers and car producers that 'consumers are just not interested in environmentally friendly cars'. However, desk research by Lane (2005) puts a different slant on this paradox. First of all, many buyers assume there are no major differences in fuel efficiency within the

TABLE 9.1 Factors mentioned as being important in the purchasing decision.

Source: Lane 2005

Most important (10–30%)	(5–10%)	Least important (< 5%)
Price	Performance and power	Depreciation
Fuel consumption	Image and style	Personal experience
Size and practicality	Brand name	Sales package
Reliability	Insurance costs	Dealership
Comfort	Engine size	**Environment**
Safety	Equipment levels	**Vehicle emissions**
Running costs		Road tax
Style and appearance		Recommendation
		Alternative fuel

same vehicle class. By buying a new car, consumers automatically assume that it has good energy efficiency and is in compliance with strict environmental norms. It is also still widely believed that an environmental choice involves a certain sacrifice: in comfort, in performance or financially. Furthermore, because consumers' knowledge is incomplete the environmental effects of car use are often confusing and complex for consumers. The relationship between fuel efficiency, CO_2 emissions and climate change is only very generally understood. Finally, the differences between local and global emissions are often mixed up.

Different environmental information tools and taxation schemes have been developed over the years in order to help consumers take environmental aspects into account when purchasing a car. Indeed, these strategies were specifically designed to tackle exactly the above-mentioned problems and misconceptions. However, clearly not all of these points have been solved. Before we investigate how these environmental tools have worked out in practice we will take a look at how these consumer-oriented strategies have been developed. As the energy-efficiency label is by far the most well-known environmental tool, the focus of the analysis will be on this label.

9.1.3 Case history and development: Dutch consumer-oriented strategies in car purchasing

In 1996 the European Commission formulated a regulation to improve overall fuel-efficiency of European cars. This regulation was based on three pillars, each with a different strategy: (1) a provider-oriented strategy based on voluntary agreements (which recently has been transfused into strict emission targets of 130 grams per kilometre of CO_2 by 2012 for an average new car); (2) a consumer-oriented labelling directive and (3) permission for member states to develop fiscal incentives for fuel-efficient cars. The EU labelling Directive stated that, from 18 January 2001 onwards, all displayed new cars should be labelled, providing information about the fuel economy and CO_2 emissions. This was explicitly presented as a consumer-oriented strategy, focusing on changing consumer choice, that would work well in conjunction with the supply-driven voluntary agreements (interview: Zierock, 2004).[4] As the member states could not agree on the exact format of the label,[5] the EU implemented the directive on the basis of minimum harmonisation. The minimum requirements were (1) the use of a label on new passenger cars that are for sale, (2) a poster in the showroom that contains information about the fuel economy of the different vehicles, (3) the provision of a fuel economy guide, with information of all vehicles for sale in the country

---

4 Details of interviews are given at the end of this chapter, after the references.
5 It did with, for example, Directive 92/75/EEC on the labelling of domestic appliances (Van den Burg 2006).

concerned and (4) that all advertisements should contain information about car fuel economy. All these displays of information at least contain the official[6] fuel consumption and the official emissions of CO_2 but the exact shape that labels should take were to be decided on by the member states.[7]

9.1.3.1 The period 1996–2001: negotiating the Dutch fuel-efficiency label

Already in 1996, when the first plans for a fuel-economy label were made, the Dutch Ministry of Environment sought contact with different interest groups. This ranged from interest groups representing the automobile sector (the RAI association and BOVAG) and the Dutch Automobile Association (ANWB) to consumer organisations (Consumentenbond) and environmental non-governmental organisations (NGOs) (Stichting Natuur en Milieu). The label as proposed by the Dutch Ministry for Environment was clearly based on a number of assumptions of what consumers wanted (Energieverwertungsagentur 1999). It was believed that consumers would not understand the parameter 'gCO$_2$/km' and the idea was brought up to develop a label that, analogous to the European label on domestic appliances, classifies cars with colours (see Fig. 9.2). The next question was whether this should be on the basis of their absolute or relative performance. It was argued that consumers, when considering purchasing a new car, have already decided on the size of the car. Fuel-efficiency labels would never convince a potential BMW buyer to switch to a Fiat Panda. Consequently, illustrating relative differences in environmental performance between comparable cars was believed more useful than absolute figures. Furthermore, an absolute label would blur the differences between cars of similar size: small cars would always do well, bigger cars never.

Industry representatives opposed the label, arguing that the process of selling and buying a car was (and should continue to be) an 'emotional experience' in which 'rational' arguments should not and will not play a role (interview: Zijlstra, 2004). Drawing on stated-preference research, they argued that, for the consumer, environmental considerations were of marginal influence (Muconsult 2000).

A fierce political struggle ensued. The Minister of Environment personally favoured the label and found the main consumer organisation (Consumentenbond), environmental organisations as well as the Dutch Automobile Association (having overcome its initial scepticism) were on his side. The matter was settled in parliament, which supported the minister. Industry representatives quickly changed tactics, acknowledging that a label could benefit (at least some)

---

6 'Official' here means the information as calculated by the European approval authority.
7 Some of these requirements have been cancelled over time.

FIGURE 9.2 The Dutch fuel-efficiency label

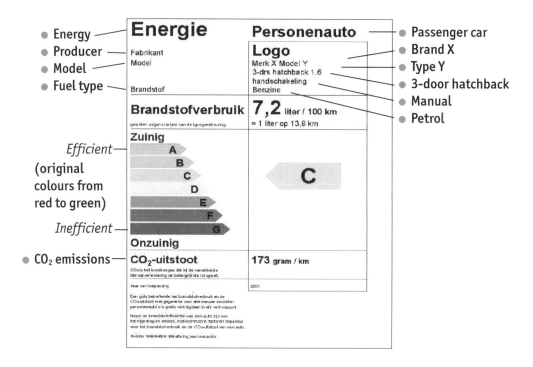

Key to colour classification:

A: at least 20% more efficient than reference norm

B: 10–20% more efficient than reference norm

C: 0–10% more efficient than reference norm

D: 0–10% less efficient than reference norm

E: 10–20% less efficient than reference norm

F: 20–30% less efficient than reference norm

G: at least 30% less efficient than reference norm

Reference norms are calculated at 25% on absolute comparison of CO_2 emissions and at 75% on relative comparison of vehicle size.

manufacturers. The subsequent (lengthy) discussion focused on the best methodology to categorise different car classes and to calculate the relative performance. The result was a formula based on length and width of the car, and its relative and absolute fuel efficiency. The 'average' car is between a C and a D label, and other cars would be compared with this standard.[8]

8 Each year, the average is recalculated and car fuel-efficiency categories are thus 'moving targets'.

9.1.3.2 The period 2002–2003: introducing a tax subsidy, and abolishing it

When the label was developed, it met severe cynicism from various parties who believed that a label would never change consumer behaviour. The hostile attitude towards labelling among industry changed when the government introduced a subsidy for A- and B-labelled cars in 2002. Consumers who bought A- and B-labelled cars received, respectively, €1,000 and €500 from the tax authorities. The industry supported this decision, keeping in mind that it was not unlikely that consumers would spend this rebate on car luxuries (interview: Zijlstra, 2004). The subsidies lasted only one year, as a newly elected conservative government decided to end this financial provision. In an unlikely collaboration, industry representatives, consumer organisations and environmental organisations jointly lobbied to maintain the subsidies, without result (interview: Clausing, 2004).

For some years after this there was very little attention given to the label. It was present in the showrooms but, apart from that, there were no organisations that actively promoted the label. Environmental NGOs undertook no activities to make the general public familiar with the label, as they claimed that others were in a better position to do so (interview: Fransen, 2004) or that they 'want to approach people as citizens, not as consumers' (interview: Ten Kate, 2004).

9.1.3.3 The period 2005–2007: increasing interest (and reopening the discussion)

Recently, this situation has changed. Very influential was the decision by the Dutch government to link the label to fiscal instruments again. In 2004 a tax subsidy specifically designed to facilitate the introduction of hybrid cars was initiated. A massive €9,000 tax decrease was provided to compensate for the higher purchase price of hybrid cars (this amount was reduced to €6,000 in 2007, partly because of pressure from European car manufacturers, who have no hybrid cars on the market). Furthermore, rising fuel prices and more attention on global warming led to a renewed interest in the label. In 2006 the purchase tax of all cars was made dependent on the energy label of the vehicle (see Table 9.2).

At the same time, a number of initiatives by governments, NGOs and corporations were undertaken. Pressurised by local governments, which drew on experiences from Germany, the national government passed legislation that allowed municipalities to differentiate parking tariffs, where a more polluting car pays more to park. Various non-state organisations also took the initiative to promote the label. The Dutch Automobile Association now provides an overview of the fuel efficiency of all vehicles on its website.[9] Despite its support for the label, the

9 www.anwb.nl/auto/dagwaarde

TABLE 9.2 Dutch taxation scheme for new cars

	Energy class						
	A	B	C	D	E	F	G
From 2004 to 1 July 2006							
Hybrid car (€)	9,000	–	–	–	–	–	–
Non-hybrid car (€)	–	–	–	–	–	–	–
July 2006–February 2008							
Hybrid car (€)	–6,000	–3,000	–	+135	+270	+405	+540
Non-hybrid car (€)	–1,000	–500	–	+135	+270	+405	+540
February 2008 onwards							
Hybrid car (€)	–6,400	–3,200	–	+400	+800	+1,200	+1,600
Non-hybrid car (€)	–1,400	–700	–	+400	+800	+1,200	+1,600

ANWB has been active in developing an alternative to the fuel-efficiency label. Together with the German automobile association, it has developed the Eco Test (see Box 9.1). The main difference is that the Eco Test also provides information on emissions other than CO_2. The fuel-efficiency label, they argue, is a over-simplification when providing information about the environmental performance of vehicles.

Box 9.1 Background on Eco Test

The Eco Test has been developed by ADAC, the German automobile association, with funding from the global FIA (Fédération Internationale de l'Automobile) Foundation. The aim of the Eco Test is to provide consumer information on aspects of the environmental performance of popular car models in Europe. Pollutants and CO_2 emissions are measured in a specially designed test. The pollutants are measured absolutely, whereas CO_2 emissions are measured relatively, depending on the vehicle class. These two values are added on an equal basis, resulting in a number (from 0 to 100) and a star rating (from 1 to 5 stars).

Other environmental organisations also changed tactics and now explicitly target cars as well. As part of a larger campaign to provide consumers with information about the environmental performance of products, the website www.hier.nu (accessed 17 March 2009) provides an 'Eco Top 10' of most energy-efficient cars in various car classes (see Box 9.2). Furthermore, the label and above-mentioned campaigns are nowadays actively used in the promotional campaigns of manufacturers, for example Daihatsu and Toyota, who actively promote their cars as an environmentally friendly alternative.

Box 9.2 Background on Eco Top 10

The Eco Top 10, which is part of the Hier campaign, offers an outline of various energy-efficient household appliances. It is comparable to Eco Top 10s developed in Germany, Switzerland, Austria and France. The Hier campaign involves 40 (inter)national charity organisations, government organisations and businesses who have formed a collective communication campaign. Similar to the Eco Test (see Box 9.1) the cars are divided into different classes. Information is given not only about environmental indicators but also about general characteristics such as storage space, purchase price and so on. Furthermore, a special feature is an indication of fuel costs (in euros per 15,000 km) of the Top 10 cars which is compared with the same indication for a very inefficient car in the same class.

9.2 Results

9.2.1 Main results: an analysis at the consumption junction

Before turning to an impact analysis of the consumer-oriented strategies mentioned above, first an insight is given into micro-level dynamics at the 'consumption junction' in new car purchasing. The consumption junction (Schwartz-Cowan 1987) is the specific time and place that a consumer makes a choice between competing products. This junction is made up of several settings that form the contact points between different rationalities: those of the consumer interested in purchasing a car, those of the car salesperson trying to sell a car and those of policy-makers and environmental NGOs trying to 'green' consumer car purchases. In this section we highlight the most important results from focus group research with Toyota car salespeople and recent Toyota purchasers.

During these focus groups we investigated how these consumer tools are assessed and evaluated by these two important actors.[10]

9.2.1.1 Consumer preferences

The results from the car salespeople focus group indicate a shift in consumer preferences over the years. The salespeople perceived that consumer interest has increased over the years as more and more questions in the showroom are environmentally related. Furthermore, the salespeople mentioned that the provision of environmental information is a tool that has potential. For one thing, the salespeople found that the EU energy-efficiency label is recognised by a large number of customers. The salespeople made a comparison with the Euro NCAP crash test to indicate how consumer demand can influence production design. Nevertheless, the salespeople remain sober and sceptical about (information concerning) environmental factors being enough to convince consumers to buy sustainable cars. Overall, environmental aspects were considered foremost as additional factors—as a bonus. The overall view is that for consumers sustainability is only an issue when it does not negatively influence the price of a car.

To a large extent this view was supported by the consumer focus group. Next to brand and dealer loyalty, the factors price, comfort, safety, reliability, space and appearance were mentioned as key decision features. However, over a third of the participants of the focus group stated that they took fuel efficiency and emissions into account.

9.2.1.2 Assessment of the Dutch energy-efficiency label

The car salespeople were positive about the effectiveness of the tax subsidy, but only with regard to small, less expensive cars where a €1,000 discount really can make a difference. On the whole, the efficiency label elicited heavy negative emotions from the car salespeople. The current system of labelling was negatively evaluated for major reasons:

- The energy label gives information only about the energy use of a new car without taking into account other environmental impacts, such as impact on local air quality. Investments in clean diesel technology are therefore not rewarded

- The division into different energy categories was found hard to understand. The complex calculations sometimes lead to contradictory situations. The sales manager gave an example of a compact-build car that

---

10 A more detailed account of the analysis at the consumption junction is provided in Nijhuis (forthcoming).

was negatively affected by this calculation because it fell into a smaller car class than its rivals. Instead of a C label the same car gets a D label because it is built smart

- In relation to the previous point, the fact that a big car can get a more positive label than a small car was seen as sending out a confusing message. Therefore, the salespeople found the energy-efficiency label impossible to communicate to consumers

As a consequence of this negative evaluation, the car salespeople openly admitted that they avoid talking about the energy label in the showroom. One strong statement of the sales trainer sums up these points: 'That is the conclusion, I think. You talk around the label and continue with other subjects.'

In the consumer focus group the subsidy was also mentioned on different occasions as a decisive factor in the purchase decision. Furthermore, all consumers were aware of the existence of the energy label and of its presence in the showroom. This means that one important prerequisite for the effectiveness of the label, that consumers must first notice the label, has been fulfilled. At first, the reaction to the energy label was generally very positive. However, at a certain point it became apparent that none of the participants knew about the relative energy classes within the label. This means that none of the purchasers had understood precisely how the label works. When this was brought to the attention of the consumer focus group the positive feelings of the consumer altered to a certain extent. First, they felt that the relativity of the classes is not clearly communicated on the energy label (and the salespeople focus group showed it is unlikely that this information is given in the showroom itself). Second, some consumers felt almost deceived by the confusing message of the label.[11]

9.2.1.3 Assessment of new environmental information tools

In Section 9.1.3.3 the development of new purchase tools, initiated by non-state actors was described. Boxes 9.1 and 9.2 describe these environmental information tools in a little more detail. During the research period the Eco Top 10 and the Eco Test were available only on the website of the corresponding providers. More recently, the Eco Top 10 has been taken as part of the marketing campaign of Toyota Netherlands.

Both the Eco Test and the Eco Top 10 were hardly known by the salespeople. Likewise, the recent car purchasers were almost completely unaware of these

---

11 A clear conclusion on consumer preference with regard to the energy label is not easy to make. Both in the car purchasers' focus group and in a conducted consumer survey, mixed reactions were given. In the consumer survey 44% of the survey respondents thought the current system was favourable, 32% found the current system lacking in clarity and 21% had no clear preference.

tools. This may be the result of their new introduction (though the Eco Test is by now five years old). Another plausible explanation is that this lack of familiarity with these tools stems from the fact that neither is available in the showroom itself. With regard to the assessment, the reactions on the Eco Test were far from positive, both in the purchasers' and in the salesperson focus group. The salespeople dismissed this tool directly by stating that it is 'completely hopeless'. In the consumer focus group the reactions were not much warmer. For instance, there was a lot of confusion related to the distinction between CO_2 points and pollution points and how they were calculated (no extra information is given about the calculation on the website). Furthermore, the long list of numbers was found to be far from attractive.

The Eco Top 10 did not fare much better than the Eco Test in car salespeople's assessments. The salespeople were quite sceptical about it; those who had seen the Eco Top 10 found it a very disputable tool. Nevertheless, the consumers responded much more positively to the Eco Top 10. The fact was appreciated that the Top 10 provided not only environmental information on CO_2 emissions and fuel costs but also other relevant information such as price and volume.

9.2.2 Change in sustainability performance

In this section we concentrate on the sustainability impact analysis of the environmental information tools and taxation schemes. The focus is predominantly based on sales of hybrid cars and developments in market shares of A-labelled and B-labelled cars from 2001 to 2007.[12] The trends shows some interesting but mixed results about the effectiveness of the Dutch consumer strategies (Table 9.3; Fig. 9.3). The number of A-labelled cars is small (5%) but has been increasing slowly over the years. With regard to the taxation scheme, there is a clear decrease in sales of A- and B-labelled cars since the abolition of the subsidy in 2002. We mentioned in Section 9.1.3.3 that in 2005 a renewed interest in the labelled could be witnessed. This is also reflected in the number of cars sold.[13] The tax subsidy of €1,000 (from 1 July 2006 onwards) has had a positive effect on the sales of A-labelled cars. An interesting remark here is that, in the first half of 2006, Toyota and Citroën privately subsidised an A-labelled model (the Toyota Aygo and the Citroën C1, respectively) in advance of the tax subsidy. The decrease in sales of B-labelled cars, however, is difficult to assess. Though not

---

12 Important to note is that these are aggregated numbers that include sales of lease cars. In The Netherlands between 30% and 35% of newly sold cars are lease cars. Furthermore, it is obvious that developments, external to the consumer-oriented strategies discussed, continue to strongly influence new car sales. We should therefore remain cautious in drawing direct causal relations between the trends and the consumer-oriented strategies.

13 The increase in the number of A- and B-labelled cars in 2005 must also be partly attributed to a more lenient calculation method (PBL 2009).

TABLE 9.3 Number of new cars sold per energy class in The Netherlands

Source: Rijksdienst voor het Wegverkeer (RDW), 2007

Energy class	Year						
	2001	2002	2003	2004	2005	2006	2007
A	1,689	14,229	6,295	5,308	16,185	24,262	29,152
B	87,182	79,250	69,366	69,299	95,869	74,270	84,759
C–G	441,360	415,263	413,316	409,278	320,490	389,162	384,371
Unknown						996	
Total	530,231	508,742	488,977	483,885	432,544	488,690	498,282

FIGURE 9.3 Market shares of new cars per energy class (A, B and C–G) in The Netherlands

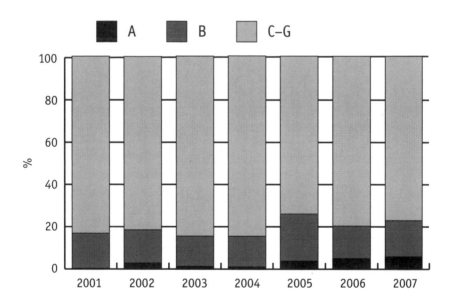

included in the graphs, recent car sales point to a substantial increase in the number of A- and B-labelled cars in 2008. The newly introduced taxation scheme not only provides a higher subsidy for sustainable cars, it simultaneously places a significantly stronger levy on unsustainable cars. Though one should be careful to claim a direct and causal relationship, it is likely that the new scheme played an important role in the stark increase (from 5% to 11%) of A-labelled cars in just one year. Similarly, the percentage of B-labelled cars has increased from 16% to 28% (for recent figures, see www.milieucentraal.nl).

The enormous influence of price mechanisms can be illustrated by taking a closer look at the sales of the Toyota Prius, by far the most sold hybrid car in The Netherlands (Table 9.4). We can see that there was virtually a non-existent market for this car before 2004. After the introduction of the special tax subsidy, as described in Section 9.1.3.3, the sales increased rapidly. A complicating matter is that the increase in sales is also the result of the introduction of the Prius II. The new Prius had a much more attractive design and was marketed not as an environmentally friendly car but intentionally as an innovative and high-tech car of the future (interview: Versteege, 2006). In four years time only 486 Prius I cars were sold whereas three years later more than 5,000 Prius II cars were sold. However, the hybrid market collapsed the month after the tax was reduced to €6,000 from the previous €9,000 (in June 2006 some 500 Priuses were sold, whereas from July onwards this was reduced to around 50). The price difference between the Prius and comparable cars apparently had become too large for consumers. In a reaction to these decreasing results Toyota Netherlands reduced the price of the Prius by €2,000 in February 2007. The sales in 2007 later recovered. More noteworthy is the enormous increase in Prius sales in 2008. This is primarily the result of two additional fiscal measures which also explicitly target the car leasing market. In The Netherlands consumers who make use of a company lease car are charged a monthly payment based on the net catalogue price of the car. In 2008 highly fuel-efficient cars (maximum of 110 g CO_2 per km) received a substantial reduction on this monthly charge. In addition, the vehicle excise duty for these highly efficient cars was halved. As hybrid cars are one of the few car models to meet these criteria, consumer interest in these cars greatly increased.

TABLE 9.4 Sales of Toyota Prius in The Netherlands

Source: Bovag

2002	2003	2004	2005	2006	2007	2008
63	18	1,107	2,736	2,388	2,229	6,415

To assess the reduction in environmental effects since the introduction of the energy-efficiency label the sales figures in Table 9.3 have to be translated in CO_2 reductions. The calculations have been done by Milieu Centraal, a Dutch NGO providing objective environmental consumer information, which has measured aggregated CO_2 reductions (see Table 9.5).[14] The basis of these calculations is

14 We are much indebted to Jan-Tjemme van Wieringen for his calculations and figures on car sales.

TABLE 9.5 Cumulative CO_2 reduction since 2001 as a result of the purchase of A-labelled and B-labelled cars in preference to C-labelled and D-labelled cars

Source: Jan-Tjemme van Wieringen, personal communication

Year	A-labelled cars		B-labelled cars	
	No. sold	CO_2 reduction (kg)	No. sold	CO_2 reduction (kg)
2001	1,689	703,469	87,182	21,185,226
2002	14,229	7,333,316	79,250	61,628,202
2003	6,295	15,881,562	69,366	97,741,890
2004	5,308	20,714,211	69,299	131,437,485
2005	16,185	29,666,046	95,869	171,573,309
2006	24,262	46,512,221	74,270	212,917,086

the knowledge that A- and B-labelled cars are, respectively, at least 20% and 10–20% more fuel-efficient than C- or D-labelled cars. Other factors (such as fuel type and kilometres driven, etc.) were based on Dutch averages. These figures point out that in the period from 2001 to 2006 there has been a reduction of approximately 260 kton of CO_2 as a result of the purchase of new cars with a greater energy efficiency than cars of the same car class.[15]

9.2.3 Learning experiences

The focus groups show that there is a clear need for help in reducing the complexity of the environmental information in the car-buying process. Currently, most information is abstract and hard to understand, whereas consumers should be stimulated and encouraged to compare cars at the level of sustainability. While one would expect consumer knowledge about the fuel economy label to have increased since 2006 (the year of the focus group research), recent studies do not support this. On the contrary, a stated preference research conducted by The Netherlands Assessment Agency shows that knowledge of the label is limited to owners of A-labelled cars (PBL 2009). On the basis of the results from the focus groups we can distil three general conditions that promote the successful use of environmental information in the purchase of new cars. First, environmental

---

15 As mentioned before, these reductions must be seen as only indicative. First, a causal relation to the consumer-oriented strategies is hard to determine. Second, 't is based on the assumption that consumers who bought A- or B-labelled cars would normally purchase C- or D-labelled cars.

information that is actively provided in the search process of consumers is more likely to be accessed. This means that these tools should be actively provided to potential purchasers in the places that matter, such as the showroom (also important are the websites of car producers, automobile associations and car magazines). Second, consumer interest increases when this information is communicated in an attractive and comprehensible way. Third, it is important that this information be provided and/or supported by a 'trustworthy' source. The showroom, and the salespeople that work there, obviously can play a decisive role in stimulating the purchase of sustainable cars and providing information about the environmental impact of the car. However, the salespeople see sustainability primarily as a bonus and not as a stand-alone selling point. Furthermore, little information in the showroom is available that points consumers to environmental aspects. The energy label, which is present because it is compulsory, clearly has not bridged this gap, not least because salespeople have no real incentive to direct consumers' attention to the label. On the contrary, because profit margins on new cars are so slim (see Section 9.1.2.1) salespeople are stimulated to sell as many extras as possible, including bigger engines. The need to change behaviour is therefore present at both the consumer and the provider side.

The sustainability impact analysis indicates that the energy label and the accompanying taxation scheme might have been influential in stimulating market demand for energy-efficient cars. On the one hand, the taxation scheme can be seen as a catalyst for change. Especially for hybrid cars, car sales show an almost direct relationship with the introduction and size of the tax subsidy. Also, for the smaller car segment a subsidy of €1,400 or €700 can be a substantial and decisive factor. On the other hand, the tax subsidy or penalty in the bigger car segments is negligible (an average new car costs about €25,000). The fact that the final catalogue price is a concoction of many different components (see Section 9.1.2.1) also makes it easy for car dealers to make the levies less visible (MMG Advies 2008). In addition, the relationship between the different label classes (A–G) and the size of the car (mini, compact, executive, etc.) is important. While the goal of the Dutch version of the fuel economy label, with its classes based on relative performance, was to provide an action perspective for each car size (see Section 9.1.3.1), in practice by far the majority of A- and B-labelled cars were to be found among the smaller car sizes. The stated preference research conducted by the Netherlands Assessment Agency shows that there is a clear mismatch between the supply of A- and B-labelled cars on offer and consumer preferences for medium- to large-sized vehicles (PBL 2009).

9.3 Potential for diffusion and scaling up

This chapter began by stating that an increasing number of consumer-oriented strategies are being initiated that make use of consumers as agents of change. These strategies are based on ideas of political modernisation in which typical command-and-control policies and legislation are replaced, or at least complemented, by so-called new environmental policy instruments, which should achieve greater effectiveness and are more democratic. In this regard, Mol speaks of 'informational governance' as the production, the processing, the use and the flow of—as well as the access to and the control over—information which is increasingly becoming vital in environmental governance (Mol 2008). This spread is also occurring with the energy label. Recently, the Dutch Minister for Housing, Spatial Planning and the Environment received the first energy-efficiency label for houses; the energy label is thus spreading to a new consumption domain, again.

However, environmental governance through these new consumer strategies is not without its limits. First, consumers are free to decide in a market economy. Too much market interference (either through informational or financial incentives) does not fit well with liberal standpoints. Second, in relation to the previous point, one can place significant question marks over technological subsidies. From the introduction of the Prius until the evaluation of the current taxation scheme in July 2008, the Dutch government subsidised the Toyota Prius with an astounding €100 million. Furthermore, the technology subsidy has resulted in a peculiar situation where an SUV (such as the Lexus RX400 Hybrid, a car that emits 192 gram CO_2 per km) receives an environmental subsidy of €3,000. Third, when looking at direct change in consumer purchase practices, the findings might to some be considered disappointing. Furthermore, a sceptic would say that environmental information tools will not persuade a consumer who is not interested in environmental aspects to purchase a green car. On the basis of an European-wide analysis of the fuel economy label, ADAC (2005) concludes that the main source of CO_2 reductions from new cars are technical developments.

However, two points are of importance here. First, in The Netherlands interesting developments are taking place that might point to a changing situation. In contrast to European-wide conclusions made by ADAC (2005) and TNO (2006)—which mentioned a lack of green car advertisements, and a lack of consumer interests in green cars—in The Netherlands we see different developments. Consumers are asking more and more environmentally related questions in the showroom. Car advertisements are actively promoting the environmental aspects of new cars, sometimes even by forming an alliance with environmental NGOs, such as in the case of the Eco Top 10. The second point is that the impact of consumer strategies and the correlating consumer purchase practice is greater than the direct environmental change. Citizen-consumers exert influence through their various identities; they exert direct influence through consumption choices, but are also represented in the development of governance arrangements and are imagined in the minds of business leaders (Van den Burg 2006). The case of the European efficiency label has shown that the introduction of the label not only means that consumers make different choices; it also means that producers make different choices.

9.4 Overall conclusions

To understand the impact of a label and its potential for upscaling there is a need to look at policy processes as well as at the actual social practice at the consumption junction. The physical and virtual sites at the consumption junction, where labels are displayed and used, influence the actual impact of labels. By now it might be clear that this dual analysis of consumer-oriented strategies in new car purchasing, which formed the heart of this chapter, cannot claim that this case is a clear success or failure. We will shortly elaborate on this viewpoint.

When we look at the policy processes in the development of the Dutch fuel-efficiency label some important points can be identified. First, we see how the exact form of the label is 'negotiated' by various involved actors. An important argument that actors draw on is that they know what 'the consumer' wants. As actors develop their perspective on the wishes of the consumer, commonly referring to research conducted, they draw on certain ideas of how consumers make choices (in this case, the process through which consumers decide to purchase a car), what kind of information they can and cannot understand and the issues that are of interest to consumers. Needless to say, such perspectives cannot be seen apart from the interests of these organisations themselves.

Bringing such debates to a closure can be difficult. In this case, the minister personally stood up to support the label, but government regulation does not necessarily end contestation of the label as 'competing' labels are being developed. Despite these contestations, the current fuel-efficiency label is still the dominant label. This cannot be explained solely because the label is compulsory by law; it also depends on the 'embedding' of the label in society. The notion of embedding refers to the number of actors who use the label, and the number of instances in which the label is used because, by doing so, the label is reproduced and justified. In the first years of its existence, all legal requirements were fulfilled but not many additional organisations used it. In recent years, the label can be found more often, for example, on websites of various NGOs, but it is also more clearly linked to other policy measures, particularly financial, measures. Figuratively speaking, a network of organisations and policy measures is created that revolves around the label. This not only justifies the label—making it harder for competing labels to gain ground—but also determines the influence that a label has.

Once a label is successfully embedded, it exerts power through various mechanisms. It puts a spotlight on the issue of fuel efficiency—for example, by allowing for the easy 'naming and shaming' of car producers—affecting the reputation of companies. Also, labels gently direct producers' attention to issue of concern, with the 'threat' of changing consumer behaviour in the background. As such, labelling also exerts influence prior to consumer choice by directing corporations to develop and market different products. A structural effect of labelling was that car manufacturers brought fuel-efficient models on the Dutch market that had not been for sale beforehand (interviews: Zijlstra, 2004; Peereboom, 2004). Also, recent studies are moderately positive about the influence of the financial incentives on the increase in sales of fuel-efficient cars (MMG Advies 2008; PBL 2009).

Though it is swiftly changing, the dominant view among policy-makers and industry representatives is still that environmental considerations are believed to play a very minor role in decisions on car purchasing. Type, price, colour, distinction and so on are all considered to be more important (interviews: Zuidgeest, 2004; Zijlstra, 2004; Clausing, 2004; Peereboom, 2004). On the one hand, this is confirmed by the consumer focus group, where consumers first mentioned these aspects as being most important. It also explains why the Volkswagen Lupo 3L (and the Toyota Prius I, as discussed in Section 9.2.2) was never a real success. The Lupo 3L was stripped of comfort and luxury (no power steering, electric windows or electric locking) to reduce car weight while at the same time the price was higher than its 'regular' counterpart. Only a small niche exists for these types of notable environmentally friendly cars that directly interfere with the dominant trend of increasing comfort in car purchasing. It is therefore not surprising that consumers considered this 'too big a sacrifice for the environment'. On the other hand, this dominant view is an oversimplification that suggests that the success of a label depends only on the question of whether or not it is taken into consideration by consumers. To understand the impact of a label, one should investigate how it is developed, how consumers' interests are articulated, the extent to which the label is contested and the ways in which it is embedded in society. For instance, the results presented in this chapter show that current information tools have not successfully assisted in reducing the complexity of the environmental information displayed. Furthermore, as this research shows, these processes do not end once a label is introduced. In order for consumption practices to become more sustainable, consumers must incorporate new forms of information, new ideas and new products into their existing practices. Companies, as the main providers of new products such as energy-efficient cars, are crucial for the success of that incorporation process and therefore should develop an active consumer orientation (Spaargaren and Van Koppen 2009). Currently we can see that car companies in The Netherlands have become much more active in using the fuel economy label and the various financial incentives in their advertising campaigns.

Finally, we have shown that the right financial incentives, especially with the support of market and civil society actors, can be very influential in greening consumers' car choices. However, the case also indicates that simple fiscal measures are not a simple panacea that works in all circumstances.

References

ADAC (Allgemeiner Deutscher Automobil Club) (2005) *Study on the Effectiveness of Directive 1999/94/EC Relating to the Availability of Consumer Information on Fuel Economy and CO_2 Emissions in Respect of the Marketing of New Passenger Cars: Final Report to the European Commission* (Munich: ADAC).

Boardman, B., N. Banks, H.R. Kirby, S. Keay-Bright, B.J. Hutton and S.G. Stradling (2000) *Choosing Cleaner Cars: The Role of Labels and Guides. Final Report on Vehicle Environmental Rating Schemes* (Oxford/Edinburgh, UK: TRI [Transport Research Institute]/ECI [Environmental Change Institute], University of Oxford/Napier University).

EC (European Commission) (1999) *Labelling Directive (1999/94/EC)*.

Energieverwertungsagentur (1999) *Labelling and its Impact on Fuel Efficiency and CO_2 Reduction: Study for the Directorate General for Energy (DGXVII) of the Commission of the European Communities* (Vienna: Energieverwertungsagentur).

Greene, D.L. (1998) 'Why CAFE worked', *Energy Policy* 26: 595-613.

Johansson-Stenman, O., and P. Martinsson (2006) 'Honestly, why are you driving a BMW?', *Journal of Economic Behaviour and Organisation* 60: 129-46.

Klein, L.R., and G.T. Ford (2003) 'Consumer Search for Information in the Digital Age: An Empirical Study of Prepurchase Search for Automobiles', *Journal for Interactive Marketing* 17: 29-49.

Lambert-Pandraud, R., G. Laurent and E. Lapersonne (2005) 'Repeat Purchasing of New Automobiles by Older Consumers: Empirical Evidence and Interpretations', *Journal of Marketing* 69: 97-113.

Lane, B. (2005) *Car Buyer Research Report: Consumer Attitudes to Low Carbon and Fuel-efficient Cars* (Bristol, UK: Ecolane Transport Consultancy).

MMG Advies (2008) *Evaluatierapport: Werkgroep evaluatie energielabel en bonus-malusregeling BPM 2006* (Den Haag: MMG Advies BV).

Mol, A.P.J. (2008) *Environmental Reform in the Information Age: The Contours of Informational Governance* (Cambridge, UK: Cambridge University Press).

Muconsult (2000) *Effectiviteit van differentiatie van BPM en alternatieve maatregelen ter stimulering van de verkoop van auto's met relatief lage CO_2-uitstoot* (Amersfoort, Netherlands: Muconsult BV).

NIDO (National Initiatief voor Duurzame Ontwikkeling) (2002) *Informatie over duurzaamheid: een zoektocht* (Leeuwarden, Netherlands: NIDO).

Nieuwenhuis, P., and P. Wells (1997) *The Death of Motoring?* (Chichester, UK: John Wiley).

Nijhuis, J.O. (forthcoming) 'Consuming Mobility: Transition Processes to Sustainable Everyday Mobility from a Consumer-Perspective', PhD thesis, Environmental Policy Group, Wageningen University, Wageningen, Netherlands.

Orsato, R.J., and S.R. Clegg (2005) 'Radical Reformism: Towards Critical Ecological Modernisation', *Sustainable Development* 13: 253-67.

—— and P. Wells (2007) 'U-turn: The Rise and Demise of the Automobile Industry', *Journal of Cleaner Production* 15: 994-1,006.

PBL (Planbureau voor de Leefomgeving) (2009) *Energielabels en autotypekeuze: Effect van het energielabel op de aanschaf van nieuwe personenauto's door consumenten* (Bilthoven, Netherlands: PBL).

Reed, G., V. Story and J. Saker (2004) 'Information Technology: Changing the Face of Automotive Retailing?', *International Journal of Retail and Distribution Management* 32: 19-32.

Schwartz-Cowan, R. (1987) 'The Consumption Junction: A Proposal for Research Strategies in the Sociology of Technology', in W.E. Bijker, T.P. Hughes and T.J. Pinch (eds.), *The Social Construction of Technological Systems* (Cambridge, MA: MIT Press): 261-80.

Shove, E. (2003) *Comfort, Cleanliness and Convenience: The Social Organisation of Normality* (Oxford, UK: Berg).

Spaargaren, G., and C.S.A. (Kris) van Koppen (2009) 'Provider Strategies and the Greening of Consumption Practices: Exploring the Role of Companies in Sustainable Consumption', in L. Hellmuth and L. Meier (eds.), *The New Middle Classes: Globalizing Lifestyles, Consumerism and Environmental Concern* (Springer Netherlands): 81-100.

Teisl, M.F., C.L. Noblet and J. Rubin (2007) 'The Design of an Eco-marketing and Labelling Programme for Vehicles in Maine', in U. Grote, A.K. Basu and N.H. Chau (eds.), *New Frontiers in Environmental and Social Labeling* (Berlin: Springer): 11-35.

TNO (Netherlands Organisation for Applied Scientific Research) (2006) *Review and Analysis of the Reduction Potential and Costs of Technological and Other Measures to Reduce CO_2 Emissions from Passenger Cars: Final Report to the European Commission* (Delft, Netherlands: TNO).

TNS Emnid (2004) 'Internet gewinnt bei der fahrzeugvermittlung weiter an bedeuting', press release, 19 August 2004.

Van den Brink, R.M.M., and B. Van Wee (2001) 'Why has car-fleet specific fuel consumption not shown any decrease since 1990? Quantitative Analysis of Dutch Passenger Car-Fleet Specific Fuel Consumption', *Transportation Research Part D* 6: 75-93.

Van den Burg, S. (2006) *Governance through Information: Environmental Monitoring from a Citizen-consumer Perspective*, PhD Thesis, Environmental Policy Group, Wageningen University, Wageningen, Netherlands.

Interviews

Clausing, Pieter, ANWB (Dutch Automobile Association), Den Haag, 8 April 2004.

Fransen, Jan, Stichting Natuur en Milieu (by telephone), 30 September 2004.

Peereboom, Kees, RAI Vereniging, Amsterdam, 20 April 2004.

Ten Kate, Albert, Friends of the Earth Netherlands (by telephone), 2 September 2004.

Versteege, Frank, Manager, Car Marketing, Toyota, Raamsdonkveer, 15 July 2006.

Zierock, Karl-Heinz, European Commission, Brussels, 10 June 2004.
Zijlstra, Wybe, BOVAG, Bunnik, 17 March 2004.
Zuidgeest, Louis, Ministry of Public Housing, Spatial Planning and the Environment, Den Haag,
    10 March 2004.

10

Environmental vehicle excise duty in Sweden

Mads Borup

Technical University of Denmark, Department of Management Engineering

An environmental excise duty on cars was introduced in Sweden in 2006. Whereas annual vehicle excise duties in many countries traditionally have been based on weight or engine size, in the new system in Sweden they are directly connected to the environmental performance of the vehicles. Carbon dioxide (CO_2) emission per kilometre is the decisive parameter. The rates are, moreover, dependent on the fuel type, with lower rates for cars that can use alternative fuels such as bio fuel.

The introduction of the environmental vehicle excise duty stems from a pronounced opinion among consumers and policy-makers that the climate impacts from road transport must be radically changed and reduced and, more specifically, that public governance and regulation should support a more environmentally friendly development in this area.

With the environmental vehicle excise duty, Sweden is among the minority of countries that connects CO_2 emissions with taxes on cars. The environmental excise duty has resulted in considerable change in the patterns of car consumption. The environmental vehicle duty is an important regulatory element in attempts to reorient development in the mobility area towards the direction of sustainability.

10.1 Case description

10.1.1 Overview and background

The environmental vehicle excise duty system introduced in Sweden in 2006 basically works like this: the duty consists of a base rate of 360 Swedish krona (SKR) plus a CO_2 component of 15 SKR per gram CO_2 exceeding 100 gram per kilometre (g/km). (Note: 10 SKR is approximately equal to €1.)

This rate is for ordinary petrol passenger cars. For cars using alternative fuels such as biofuel the additional component is only 10 SKR per gramme CO_2 per kilometre. For diesel cars the amount is multiplied by 3.5. This is done in order to compensate for the generally lower tax on diesel fuel and lower requirements concerning emissions of particles, nitrogen oxides (NO_x), etc.

The resulting charge may, for example, be 1,830 SKR for a petrol car with average emissions of 198 g/km (2003 figure), or 660 SKR for a car with the relatively low emission of 120 g/km. Compared with the prices of new passenger cars, which often are in the order of 100,000–200,000 SKR or more, the duty amounts are visible though not extraordinarily large. The impact of the new, environmentally based, duties must be seen together with connected activities such as the establishment of the concept of green cars (*miljöbilar*), as described below.

The problem with emission of greenhouse gases from road transport in Sweden is significant. The weight and power of the passenger cars consumers buy have increased significantly in recent decades. Similar developments have been seen in other countries; however, the car fleet in Sweden is the heaviest in Europe, and the two manufacturers of passenger cars, Saab and Volvo, are targeted at the segment of larger cars (Kågeson 2004). Sweden is a 'car country', with the car manufacturing industry being one of the traditionally strong industries and with low taxes imposed on the acquisition of new cars.

Figure 10.1 shows the average CO_2 emissions from cars in different EU countries. Emissions from cars in Sweden are considerably higher than those in other EU countries. In 2003 the average was 198 g/km. In this sense, Sweden is 'worst in class' considering CO_2 emissions, as has been pointed out by observers. The positive tendency in the 1990s to reduce emissions stopped by the beginning of the 2000s.

As Figure 10.2 shows, the share of purchases of larger cars—more than 1,700 kg, or more than 1,500 kg—increased significantly, from 8% of new registrations in 1990 to more than 50% in 2003. Conversely, the share of registrations of small cars—less than 1,000 kg or 1,300 kg—decreased considerably, from 52% in 1990 to around 13% in 2003.

FIGURE 10.1 The development of average carbon dioxide (CO$_2$) emissions, in grammes per kilometre (g/km) from cars in selected EU countries

Source: Kågeson 2005a

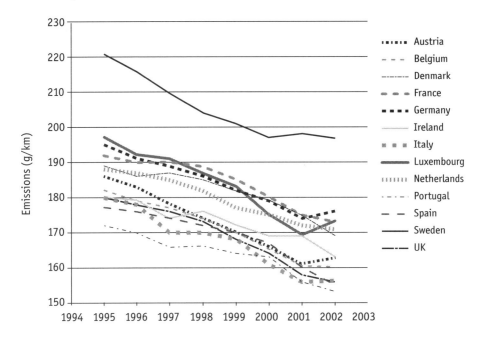

FIGURE 10.2 Development in registrations of new passenger cars in Sweden, by weight

Sources: BIL Sweden; Kågeson 2005b

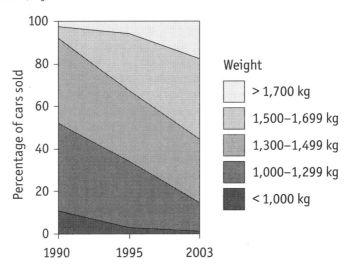

10.1.2 Actors and their roles

10.1.2.1 Primary actors

Many actors have been involved in the development of the environmental vehicle excise duty in Sweden. As a regulatory effort at national level, however, the Swedish government and the national public authorities played a very central role. The government has been actively involved in the development of the strategy and policy on the issue, with the Ministry of Sustainable Development (now the Ministry of Environment) in a leading role. Vägverket, the Swedish Road Administration, is responsible for the administration of the vehicle duties and, moreover, carries out many of the analyses behind the environmental vehicle duties.

With the increasing road traffic and the connected increasing impacts on climate and environment, the government in 2003 included the road transport sector as a central, critical, element in its climate policy and initiated the development of a climate strategy for the road transport sector (Vägverket 2004). Taxes for more CO_2-efficient vehicles and for a change to new, renewable, fuel types are among the instruments pointed out in the strategy. It is stressed that a radical change both in the short term and in the long term is needed.

Overlapping with this strategy, the government launched a radical policy against societal dependence on oil and against the existing oil regimes within the energy and transport sector (e.g. *Dagens Nyheter* 2005). The goal is to create independence from oil within 15 years and to reduce the use of oil significantly by 2020. For road transport the reductions are to be 40–50%. Apart from sustainability and climate issues this policy also concerns aspects such as international independence and self-sufficiency, industry policy, agricultural policy and regional policy. A high-level commission (which included the Prime Minister)— the Commission Against Oil Dependence—worked on the issue. Renewable energy from biomass and development of fuel-efficient cars in the 'Swedish–American' car industry are important elements of the commission's recommendations (Kommissionen mot oljeberoende 2006).

The successful establishment of the concept of 'green cars' (*miljöbiler*) is an aspect that is closely related to the effects of the environmental vehicle duty. Over recent years, the concept has been widely disseminated. It is now well known among the general public and is a term that is frequently used in mass media, public discussions and in connection with the trading of cars. The concept has become the norm and is present in the consciousness of people when discussing cars and road transport.

The official definitions of green cars by the government and national authorities have been changed and updated a couple of times (Vägverket 2005) and are continuously discussed. Many actors, such as local municipalities, representatives of the car industry, consumers and non-governmental organisations

(NGOs), have been involved in the discussions of the green car concept and there are examples of local municipalities that make their own definitions in connection with, for example, restricted access to town centres, parking charges and so on. The most recent national definition of a green car is as follows (Regeringskansliet 2007):

● Conventional cars: petrol and diesel cars with CO_2 emissions that do not exceed 120 g/km

● Alternative-fuel cars: cars that can run on fuels other than petrol or diesel and with fuel consumption that does not exceed 0.92 litres petrol per 10 km, 0.84 litres diesel per 10 km or 0.97 m^3 gas per 10 km.

● Electric cars: a passenger car meeting the so-called environmental class Mk EL standards and with electric energy consumption that does not exceed 3.7 kilowatt hours per 10 km

Though a change of government took place in 2006, the policy and strategy concerning the climate impacts from road transport has not completely changed. In Spring 2007 the new government introduced a 10,000 SKR rebate on new green cars, and the Minister of Environment expects that in his coming climate proposition there will be suggestions of higher taxes on CO_2, more expensive petrol and cheaper public transport (Ekot 2007; Regeringskansliet 2007). In 2006 a rebate of 6,000 SKR was introduced for diesel cars with reduced particle emissions (particle filters).

10.1.2.2 Other actors

A large number of organisations have been active in the establishment and discussion of environmental vehicle duties and the definitions of environmental categories of cars. The car manufacturing industry and its industry organisation, BIL Sweden, participated in much of the discussion and, among other things, argue for continued emphasis on road transport as an important part of transport infrastructure, for alternative fuels, for a technical focus on improved cars and for long planning horizons (BIL Sweden 2006). Also, representatives of car distributors, car dealers and so on have made contributions.

Environmental and consumer organisations also participated in discussions. Among consumers of cars and mobility by road there has been an increasing concern about pollution from car transport. Many find that, on the one hand, they need, or like, to use a car; on the other hand, the climate and other environmental impacts from car transport must be addressed and limited. Green Motorists (Gröna Bilister) is a consumer organisation representing such viewpoints. The organisation is active, among other things, concerning the definitions of green cars. Apart from measures for reducing the environment impacts, they have, for example, addressed issues such as the prices on the market for used cars and for interim arrangements for older cars (Gröna Bilister 2005).

A large number of consumers in Sweden support the attempts to change the climate impact of road traffic. A survey showed that about 66% of Swedish consumers will definitely choose a more environmentally friendly car next time (87% if one includes 'yes, maybe' answers). A similar share is interested in changing their way of driving to be more fuel-efficient. Moreover, around 75% of the Swedes find that they can themselves do something in order to stop the greenhouse effect and climate change: 71% answer 'yes, absolutely' or 'yes, maybe' to whether they will drive more slowly. Around 50% expect that they will use more public transport in the future and thus drive cars less (Naturvårdsverket 2006).

People's opinions on these issues have become much clearer and stronger over recent years. Whereas similar surveys in 2002 and 2003 showed considerable lack of awareness and had 'don't know' shares of 12–18% of the answers, the corresponding figures are now only 1–5%. In general, eight out of ten Swedes are interested in paying 5% more for services and products from companies that work to limit the greenhouse effect. Moreover, the public in general supports the idea that Sweden should reduce its emissions of greenhouse gases more than required by the EU. More than 90% of the population take this stance.

Changes in the understanding of the relationship between car consumption and climate are reflected in the media. The media coverage of cars is to a larger extent than before dealing with environmental issues and the environmental parameters of cars. This is another indication that climate issues are on the agenda for consumers. The green car concept, in brief, has shown to fit well to mass media communication, and media writings about green cars must be considered to have played an important role in the broad dissemination of the concept.

As mentioned, a number of connected activities and efforts have been influential on the impact of the environmental vehicle excise duty. In addition to the activities mentioned above we must also mention regional climate strategies for the road transport sector and environmentally oriented planning efforts in larger towns and cities such as Stockholm, Götenburg and Malmö. These efforts, among other things, include lower speed limits, restrictions on access and parking for cars with high emissions and, for some time, congestion charges (in Stockholm). Moreover, the towns and cities have played leading roles in the development of information material and news about green cars and transport (e.g. www.miljöfordon.se; www.stockholm.se/miljöbilar, accessed 17 March 2009).

Voluntary as well as obligatory requirements of environmental information to consumers in connection with car purchases have been established and the public authority on consumption publishes information on the issue (Konsumentverket 2006). Consumers thus often meet this information at the same time as they are considering the environmentally based vehicle excise duties. In addition, information dissemination and knowledge development about consumers' opportunities for more environmentally friendly driving (eco-driving) are undertaken.

The demand for environmentally friendly cars for public institutions and regional, local and national authorities was originally one of the arguments for defining the concept of green cars, and public procurement has played an important role in developments in the area. All these different activities have been part of the context for the environmental vehicle excise duty and must be remembered when considering the results.

10.2 Results

The environmental vehicle excise duty in Sweden has resulted in a drastic increase in the number of new green cars. The increase from July 2005 to July 2006 was 390%. Of the new cars purchased in July 2006, 12.8% were green cars. In July 2005 the figure was only 2.9%. This means that the share of green cars more than quadrupled (Klimataktuellt 2006, 2007). In April 2007, 14.3% of new cars purchased were green cars. The number of new cars with emissions of less than 120 grammes CO_2 per kilometre was three times as many in the first quarter of 2007 as in the same period the year before (Ehrenstråhle 2007; BIL Sweden 2007). The environmental duty system has thus led to considerable change in consumers' consumption patterns concerning the purchasing of cars.

With these changes, the numbers of environmentally friendly cars and of cars with alternative fuels in Sweden are clearly much larger than in most other countries, including, for example, in otherwise comparable countries such as Finland, Norway and Denmark. CO_2 emissions from new cars are on average still relatively high but have, compared with the 198 g/km in 2003, improved to 191 g/km in 2006.

The consumption of petrol shows a parallel change, though there is some uncertainty concerning how much of this can be directly connected to the use of green cars (and not, for example, to changes in oil prices). From mid-2005 to mid-2006 petrol consumption in Sweden decreased by 3.6%. Instead, the consumption of ethanol fuel and diesel increased. The use of ethanol fuel increased threefold but still accounts in total for only a small share of fuel use. Diesel consumption increased by 2.7% (SPI 2006).

Consumers have become increasingly concerned about and aware of the climate impact from their road transport and car driving over the past few years.

There is a clear understanding that there is need for further change if mobility patterns are to be sustainable. The establishment of the concept of green cars has been quite successful. It is a visible subject in the mass media and appears on many homepages and in the shops of car dealers. It is also highlighted on the homepages of car manufacturers. The green car classification is often an important element in the sale and purchase of cars. Whereas in 2003 'only' 52% would choose a more environmentally friendly car, in 2006 the figure is 66%. People are now more enthusiastic about eco-driving and about reducing their use of cars (Naturvårdsverket 2006).

Public procurement through the purchasing of green cars by public authorities has developed significantly. Some 62% of authorities meet the requirement of having at least 75% green cars among their new purchases. This is double the figure of 2005. In 2006, authorities bought 941 green cars. This constitutes 70% of cars in the categories addressed by the requirements (another 604 vehicles are for different reasons exempt from the requirements) (Klimataktuellt 2007).

The large Swedish-produced cars are also popular when it comes to models that can use alternative fuels. In 2006 the car manufacturers Saab and Volvo accounted for three of the top-five most sold ethanol cars in Sweden (see Table 10.1). To the car industry, the area of green cars appears to be one of the most important strategic areas of development.

TABLE 10.1 Top five ethanol cars sold in Sweden in 2006

Source: BIL Sweden 2007

Rank	Model	Number of cars sold
1	Saab 9-5	10,941
2	Ford Focus	7,237
3	Volvo V50	5,172
4	Volvo S40	1,452
5	Ford Focus C-Max	1,066

Though there are some clear, positive, tendencies in the direction of sustainable mobility, the Swedish environmental vehicle can in some senses only partly be called a success. The car fleet is still heavier and more fuel-consuming than those in other European countries and there are no clear signs that cars are used significantly less or significantly more efficiently. Moreover, the total number of new cars registered is increasing somewhat, not decreasing. It has been pointed out that, despite the higher emissions, larger cars with large motors are still popular and enjoy considerable goodwill. New cars have become more efficient, with average fuel consumption decreasing from 8.2 litres per 100 km in 2004 to 7.8 litres per 100 km in 2006 (the EU-15 average in 2004 was 6.5 litres per 100 km), but considerably more must be done in order to meet climate targets and break radically from the current development tendencies in emissions of greenhouse gases from road transport.

Although there are continued discussions about the environmental advantages of alternative fuels, environmental vehicle duties and the related efforts have clearly led to developments towards the goal of becoming less dependent on oil.

10.3 Further learning experience and conclusions

The results of the environmental vehicle excise duty have appeared at the level of broad consumer markets. In this sense, the effects of this tool have been much more far-reaching than many small-scale experiments, demonstration projects and so on. A system-level perspective is employed, explicitly expressed in the climate strategy for road transport and in the policy against oil dependence. With the ambition of making a radical break from the dominant oil regime in the areas of transport and energy (and in society in general) the case is very unusual and ambitious in its goals for system change. With regard to consumers' consumption patterns, the goal is not the elimination of road transport but a radical change in its climate impact through, among other things, a significant transformation of the cultural understanding of cars and car transport. In the new understanding, environmental performance is a key aspect. The widespread dissemination of the green car concept is central to this.

The case represents a multi-actor development in which consumers and producers of mobility solutions are actively engaged. Policy-makers and public authorities are, however, the type of actor that must be said to have played the most central role. Mass media communication and public discussion have also been very important. The important role of not only consumers and producers per se but also of organisations and associations representing them must be stressed.

At the time of this analysis, the environmental vehicle duty system had been in force for only about one year. Wider dissemination and greater effects are expected when the system has been working longer. Recent statistics support this. The amount of green cars sold has continued to increase in 2007 and 2008: from spring 2007 to spring 2008 the amount has doubled (BIL Sweden 2008). Larger dissemination and greater effects can be expected in coming years. There seem to be possibilities for further improvement of the system in the future: for example, through a continuous assessment of the criteria for the classification of green cars and fuels.

For other countries there seems to be great potential to learn from experiences in Sweden and to make similar efforts. The efforts in Sweden are, however, complex and tied to a specific context. They include many complementary activities and not just the basic introduction of a new regulation on vehicle excise duties. If one had introduced the new vehicle duty more or less 'in silence' and without the many connected activities, the results would not have been as significant.

This means that other countries should not simply copy the Swedish environmental excise duty. The considerable emphasis on individual vehicles in efforts towards sustainable mobility is probably to some extent a result of the traditionally large role of the car industry in Sweden. In other countries the weight might be placed differently: for example, with more emphasis on taxes on fuel or on the integration of public and private transport.

References

BIL Sweden (2006) *Vägtransporterna kan bli oljeoberoende* (Stockholm: BIL Sweden).

—— (2007) *Nyregistreringsstatistik från BIL Sweden, 2006–2007* (Stockholm: BIL Sweden).

—— (2008) *Nyregistreringsstatistik från BIL Sweden, 2007–2008* (Stockholm: BIL Sweden).

Dagens Nyheter (2005) 'Persson vill ha bort oljan, Reporting from the Congress of the Social Democratic Party Oct–Nov 2005', *Dagens Nyheter,* 1 November 2005; www.dn.se.

Ehrenstråhle, E. (2007) 'Miljöbilar väntas slå rekord', *E24 Näringsliv,* Stockholm, 2 April 2007; www.e24.se.

EKOT (2007) *Miljöministern: bensinskatten kan höjas* (Stockholm: Sveriges Radio, EKOT; www.sr.se/ekot, accessed 17 March 2009).

Gröna Bilister (2005) *Synspunkter från Gröna Bilister på Vägverkets preliminära miljöbilsdefinition* (Stockholm: Gröna Bilister).

Kågeson, P. (2004) *Varför är Sverige sämst i klassen? Den svenska fordonsflottan i ett europeiskt perspektiv* (Borlänge, Sweden: Vägverket).

—— (2005a) *Reducing CO$_2$ Emissions from New Cars* (Brussels: T&E, European Federation for Transport and Environment).

—— (2005b) *Väljer konsumenten framtidsbilen?* (Borlänge, Sweden: Vägverket).

Klimataktuellt (2006) *Tretton procent miljöbilar i juli* (Stockholm: Naturvårdsverket, July 2006).

—— (2007) *Allt fler miljöbilar på myndigheterna* (Stockholm: Naturvårdsverket, March 2007, building on figures from Vägverket).

Kommissionen mot oljeberoende (2006) *På väg mot ett OLJEFRITT Sverige* (*Towards an Oil-Free Sweden*) (Stockholm: Regeringskansliet).

Konsumentverket (2006) *Bilar, bränsleförbrukning och vår miljö* (Stockholm: Konsumentverket).

Naturvårdsverket (2006) *Allmänheten och växthuseffekten 2006* (Stockholm: Naturvårdsverket).

Regeringskansliet (2007) *Regeringen inför miljöbilspremie* (*The government introduces green car rebate*) (Stockholm: Ministry of the Environment).

Skatteverket (2006) 'Fordonsskattetabeller'; www.skatteverket.dk, accessed 17 March 2009.

SPI (Svenske Petroleumsinstitutet) (2006) *Bränslestatistik 2005–2006* (Stockholm: Svenska Petroleum Institutet).

Vägverket (2004) *Klimastrategi för vägtransportsektorn* (*Climate Strategy for the Road Transport Sector*) (Vägverket report 2004-06, authored by Håkon Johansson and Lars Nielsson; Borlänge, Sweden: Vägverket).

——(2005) *Rapportering av regeringsuppdrag att vidareutveckla en miljöbilsdefinition* (*Reporting of the Governmental Assignment of Further Development of the Green Car Definition*) (Borlänge, Sweden: Vägverket).

11
Conclusions
Sustainable consumption and production in the mobility domain

Theo Geerken

Flemish Institute for Technological Research (VITO), Belgium

Mads Borup

Technical University of Denmark, Department of Management Engineering

Arnold Tukker

Netherlands Organisation for Applied Scientific Research (TNO)

This chapter summarises the outcomes from the review Chapter 2 and the lessons learned from the case-study chapters, Chapters 3–10, from a system perspective. The discussion and insights developed during the two interactive mobility workshops have been condensed into sets of compact statements (included here as Boxes 11.1–11.5). They provide thoughts on mobility problems, on the factors hindering or promoting change, on the directions for a solution and on proposals for action. Actions that the triangle of change (government, business and consumers) can take in the short, medium and long term are presented.

11.1 Systemic description of the mobility domain

In this book the scope of mobility is defined as 'personal transport', both for private and for public purposes, including all modes of transport. Evidently, the car mode gets more attention because of its dominance and its associated sustainability problems (carbon dioxide [CO_2] emissions, congestion, casualties). The technological issues do not form the central theme in this book as there already exists a wide literature on such issues. The focus is more on important system elements and changes in infrastructure, vehicles or behaviour that could contribute to a sustainable consumption and production (SCP) approach in the mobility domain, building on evidence from cases.

11.1.1 The 'landscape': relevant meta-factors for mobility

Landscape meta-factors in the system approach are factors outside the mobility system as such that exert an influence from wider society on the mobility system. Mobility functions as a kind of enabling technology or service to fulfil human needs and wants for displacement. These needs and wants for mobility are determined mainly by the following meta-trends:

- Population development. Although it has grown in the past it is currently stabilising and expected to decrease in the future for Europe

- Individualisation. This leads to more households each needing mobility solutions

- Increase in double-income households. Participation rates of women in the labour market have increased considerably; each worker needs a solution to his or her commute

- Internationalisation and globalisation. The world is developing in the direction of an open international economy. This leads automatically to greater transport volumes of goods as well as to more business and leisure trips. World trade is growing even faster than the world GDP

- Urban sprawl. The majority of the population lives in urbanised areas, and many people prefer to live at the outskirts of the bigger cities, leading to urban sprawl

- Increase in welfare (through economic growth) combined with available leisure time and the perceived need to enjoy more and more frequent but shorter holidays

- The rapid developments in information and communication technology (ICT) of recent decades have also promoted new needs for (international) mobility in wider networks

Concerning environmental sustainability, we have seen a tremendous increase in attention to climate problems in recent years—in the public arena, the media and among debaters and policy-makers. We currently in an extremely exciting situation—a situation where not only mobility systems and practices may change but also the very landscape shaping the mobility area are transforming. As such we cannot predict exactly where the change will lead us; however, it seems clear that the many small balances shifted by increases in concern and awareness will together result in significant changes.

It is fair to say, as critics do, that the increased attention on climate to a large degree is mostly talk, until now. It has not yet been accompanied by similar, radical, change in consumption patterns, institutions and policy instruments used in the mobility area, but it is clear that changes will appear, most probably induced by economic arguments and worries about security of supply.

In spite of impressive results in achieving absolute decoupling of the so-called polluting emissions (carbon monoxide [CO], volatile organic compounds [VOCs], nitrogen oxides [NO_x], lead [Pb] and sulphur dioxide [SO_2]) from economic growth (and from growth in consumption levels) in car transport, the following three main sustainability issues still need solutions:

- High and still increasing contributions to global warming from car transport and strongly increasing contributions from air transport

- Increasing levels of congestion

- Slowly decreasing but still high levels of car accidents (at the EU level, and growing at the world level) with injured people or fatalities

An upcoming issue is the emission of fine particles (PM10 and PM2.5), especially from diesel engines.

Box 11.1 Statements about trends

- Mobility systems are like ICT systems; they are enabling technologies that have created much socioeconomic progress and have served our needs and wants, but they have also created new needs and wants
- Mobility has become a condition *sine qua non* in most aspects of life
- Individualisation is the most important meta-trend for the development in the mobility area, in the past and for the future
- The only environmental improvements that have led to absolute decoupling for mobility in society have been technical measures for specific emissions (low-sulphur fuel, lead-free petrol, catalytic converters, conversion from steam and diesel trains to electric trains)

11.1.2 Production–consumption mobility chain and interlinked practices: the 'regime'

The sociotechnical regime that has allowed the transport system in Western society to grow over the past century can be characterised by an interactive game with four main players:

- Authorities. These are responsible for providing and maintaining the public infrastructure for transport (although railway companies often started as private companies at the beginning of the 20th century), including all associated regulation. Authorities or public bodies are usually also responsible for the operation of public transport. Recently, the concept of privatisation as a means to increase competition and improve service levels has been introduced into public transport. Private investments in public infrastructure are also encouraged by public authorities (such as the *péage* in France) in recent years, most probably to reduce levels of public investment

- Private producers of vehicles (cars, trains, buses, airplanes, bicycles, etc.). These are free to develop and sell vehicles to customers such as consumers, companies and authorities

- Users (private and professional). These choose the best solution in terms of budget, time, quality and comfort for their own transport needs or wants

- Fuel producers and their outlets. These may provide any type of fuel

In the mobility need area authorities play a plurality of roles and are not simply market regulators between producers and consumers: (multiple) national, regional and local authorities are heavily involved and have vested interests in the regime as:

- Providers and owners of road and public transport infrastructure

- Operators of public transport services (although privatisation is starting up)

- Regulators regarding safety, traffic rules, product standards and so on

- Cashiers of fuel, vehicle and road taxes and excises (for instance, in Belgium car and fuel taxes constitute 8% of all tax income to the state)

- Public procurers of mobility

Within the general societal transport system one can identify different interlinked systems that partially use the same system components (infrastructure, vehicles, fuel):

- Transportation of goods versus transportation of people

- Public transport versus private transport

- Different system modes: air, rail, road, water

The interlinked practices between transport systems are very much entangled within society and are very complex. Sometimes they create problems (such as worsening congestion when trucks for goods and private commuters share the same roads at the same peak hours, or road congestion around centralised airports) and sometimes they provide possibilities for change (better connections between public and private transport through train, taxi, and park-and-ride stations).

11.1.3 Stabilising factors, and factors hindering change in the mobility regime

Internal changes and beneficial external changes related to the mobility regime are often not easy to achieve because of stabilising factors or factors hindering change. The factors often originate from professional, economic or social lock-in situations.

In general the transaction costs for a person to buy a new home in the EU15 vary between 4% and 19%, and this leads to reduced labour mobility (De Graaff and van Leuvensteijn 2007). In Belgium these costs are among the highest in Europe, and people buying a new home will have to pay approximately 15% of the home value in taxes, registration costs and notary fees plus an additional 3% to the real estate agent if using such a service. People having changed job to one in a location further away from their home, not being sure that the job will be satisfactory or long-lasting, face an enormous financial loss by moving house. In practice, this often leads to people continuing to live in the same home and increased demands for mobility. The Flemish authorities have recognised this economic lock-in situation and have introduced not only lower registration taxes (10% instead of 12.5%) but also a policy measure for persons already having paid registration taxes for the previous home: they get a kind of 'rucksack', the previously paid amount (to a maximum of €12,500, relating to a home value of €100,000), which does not need to be paid again. This policy has not been evaluated in terms of its effects on reduced transport mobility, but, despite lowering the registration costs, the total amount of income to the state has increased. Part of this rise in state income can be attributed to more first-time buyers (owing to the more attractive 10% rate) and another (still unknown) part can be attributed to people moving to other homes.

The mobility regime has adapted itself to all our societal regimes (labour regime, leisure regime, education regime, shopping regime, etc.), and each of these societal regimes relies on an unrestricted mobility regime.

The existing infrastructure—roads, railways, airports and the built environment (homes, offices, factories) for private and professional use—is a stabilising factor because of the economic lock-in that it creates. This leads to a high inertia towards rapid changes in system components.

For producers the economies of scale that are needed to survive competition lead to high levels of technological standardisation, making it difficult for new entrants (without protected home markets) to be competitive from scratch on a worldwide scale. For example, the Smart® car, as a newcomer, was bought by the much stronger player Daimler, which had greater engineering capacity. Past high investments in technology and infrastructure create path dependence.

Producers produced small and efficient cars but consumers did not replace the bigger cars but used them quite often as a second car. Aspects such as usability, comfort, attractive design and image have up till now seemed to have been more important than saving money on running costs and creating less environmental damage. Higher oil prices are needed for a change in this respect and the first signs of change became visible in 2007 and 2008: fuel consumption has become a clear competitive issue (judging from advertisements) as the ACEA (European Automobile Manufacturers' Association) covenant for a voluntary sector-wide reduction of CO_2 emissions per kilometre did not deliver enough results, and Europe is preparing itself for regulation.

Consumers seem to have a relatively fixed time budget for daily transport (the Brever law).Consumers cannot rapidly change their behaviour because of higher prices, which is reflected in the relative high inelasticity associated with mobility. In the short term, consumers are locked in because of their own situation and cannot significantly reduce travelling when prices rise (high price inelasticity on the short term). Only in the long term (over several years) can people adapt their needs and wants better to higher price levels (by changing the location of either their work or home, by buying a car with a lower fuel consumption level, by reducing leisure activities and so on), although as a handicap there do exist clear professional, economic and social lock-ins that lead to resistance towards this change. Furthermore, the decisions of consumers are not purely rational, and habits and routines play a stabilising role.

A factor creating uncertainty for change is the unpredictability of collective consumer behaviour in a mobility system where use is a free market, the infrastructure is the responsibility of authorities and vehicle production is a business responsibility. Infrastructure projects can only be designed first time right, as corrections are very expensive

Car ownership itself creates a kind of lock-in because of its lower price perception compared with that of public transport. Car purchase costs are to a large extent fixed (every five or ten years, say) and insurance and taxes are typically paid on a yearly basis. The variable costs for fuel and parking are the only ones felt on a per-trip basis. Consumers perceive public transport, which includes all

Box 11.2 Statements about factors hindering change

- The mobility system is often needed as a solution to our socioeconomic and professional lock-in situations

- The research on price elasticity for mobility, which exhibits a much lower short-term elasticity compared with the higher long-term elasticity, demonstrates that consumers and/or users are locked in (by routines and context) and need time to change in other areas as well

- In a democratic society, the lack of measures restricting citizens' mobility is a major barrier to change in travel patterns

- The versatility and flexibility of a car together with our societal regime make the car practically indispensable for a family household not living in a city centre or near efficient and effective public transport routes

- Car ownership creates a kind of lock-in owing to the lower price perception for a car compared with that for public transport because of the splitting-up of fixed and variable costs for cars

- A wide spread in hours to start and finish the daily job reduces congestion but also limits possibilities for big entities to promote more sustainable and also congestion-reducing collective forms of transport that need synchronised start and finish hours

- Mobility systems suffer from many lock-in situations and path dependences because of the high investments in and lifetimes of infrastructure and vehicles (especially for trains, aeroplanes and ships)

- A certain level and frequency of congestion is economically desirable for the efficient use of budgets for infrastructure (like a longer queue at peak hours in a shop)

- Without road congestion public transport would lose more users. The solving of all congestion problems will reduce environmental emissions in the short term but will lead in the long term to increased car consumption, with associated increases in emissions

- As long as policy and society is tolerant of the external effects of motorised mobility, nothing will really change with regard to the sustainability problems of such mobility

costs on a per-trip basis, as more expensive and also know that the average cost of a car kilometre goes down when used more (Hoogma 2002).

The managerial complexity of big system changes (such as the creation of a hydrogen economy) requiring many simultaneous changes from different actors at different levels within a public and a private context is also a factor hindering change (and this feeds the hope for a simple solution: a sustainable car!). This complexity also calls for smaller intermediate steps such as hydrogen experiments with buses (such as the EU CUTE project [EU 2006]) as a suitable niche application.

11.2 Potential for change

11.2.1 Factors supporting change and windows of opportunity in the system

There exists pressure from inside and outside the mobility system to change, owing to a number of driving forces. Factors supporting change, derived from the cases in the previous chapters and other background material, are:

- Contextual life-changes (residential relocation, job changes, retirement)

- Fear of oil dependence, about security of supply and about rising oil prices

- Increased awareness of health and nuisance aspects ('no pain, no change')

- Media attention leading to growing awareness of the problem of global warming

- The attractiveness of more sustainable alternatives in terms of current limiting conditions and constraints (money, time, comfort), such as the high-speed train (Brussels–London, Brussels–Paris) rapidly gaining a market share on short distances

- The increase in value and norms of more sustainable lifestyles promoted by champions and authorities leading by example

- A new (political) team to do the job

- The growth of a new governance level at the urban policy level

Box 11.3 Statements about windows of opportunity

- Patterns of business travel can be significantly changed through implementation of obligatory mobility management in companies and authorities in combination with an increased focus on ethical responsibility

- ICT could help to provide door-to-door mobility solutions and services that provide and optimal combination of collective and individual transportation modes

- Mobility regulation that builds on market-based instruments (such as tradable quota systems, carbon compensation schemes and so on) creates the potential for consumers to take opportunities to act in an environmentally responsible way, but so far the contribution of this approach has not been very significant

- In order to move towards sustainable consumption and production systems in the mobility area, support for and nursing of promising consumption niches are essential. Alliances between sustainability-minded business actors and concerned consumer groups are a key issue for sustainability changes in the mobility area

Success and failure factors for innovations in sustainable transport based on eight cases in The Netherlands (van den Bergh *et al.* 2007) have been identified and have led to the conclusion that political, process-related, sociocultural and psychological factors are the most significant to success or failure. Technical and content-related and economic factors appeared to be less important, and administrative and legal factors played an intermediate role. The European energy Agency (EEA) identified three key success factors to reduce greenhouse gas emissions in the transport sector: implementation of accompanying measures, strong leadership and the raising of awareness (EEA 2008b).

Mobility infrastructure has the character of a public good to be freely used by everybody as long as they pay for it through (in)direct taxes or tickets per usage. This has been the basic system paradigm of the free market for mobility. It is only recently that the first cracks in this free-market system (free access or access as long as you pay) have appeared, such as those introduced by local urban traffic authorities that limit access to certain parts of the infrastructure, that allow access to the city centre only for zero-emission vehicles or to even or odd number plates only on a day basis in case of heavy smog, that create lanes for carpoolers only, that exclude SUVs in city centres and so on. Also, for example, national authorities have developed mobility policies for their own employees that exclude the use of air transport for distances less than 300 km, as was announced in The Netherlands in 2008.

ICT provides opportunities not only for working at home or teleworking at satellite offices or for videoconferencing but also creates communication platforms for people having a similar need. In the case 'Work Closer to Home' (Chapter 4), a web-based tool has been developed to connect people with the same professional profile but working and living in different locations for a possible exchange of job. This experiment tries to solve both the social lock-in (not wanting to lose social capital such as friends or existing networks for all activities) and the professional lock-in arising from a lack of published vacancies. Within labour policy there can exist also lock-in situations that discourage people from moving to another job (for mobility reasons to be closer to home), such as losing money for a pension or losing seniority in their jobs (starting again at the bottom of a list of employees, risking being the first one to lose their job in an economic downturn).

11.2.2 Visions of sustainable consumption and production in the mobility domain

The three main strategies are to:

● Reduce the need for mobility

● Promote the use of the most sustainable modes: 'modal shift'

● Improve the sustainability performance of all modes

11.2.2.1 Reducing the need for mobility

Overall vision
In a free-market economy voluntary initiatives by consumers to reduce their needs have not been very successful so far, even when there are cost benefits. To intensify this strategy, promotion of sustainable meta-values is needed (through icons and champions) as well as solutions to lock-in situations (professional, social and economic) with which mobility users are confronted and which are currently limiting the possibilities of reducing the work–home distance. (Answers may be to find solutions for improved labour mobility, reducing or eliminating lock-in or perhaps finding 'lock-out' tax policies, and spatial planning based on a long-term mobility vision.) In fact, this strategy requires changes outside the mobility system in many other societal systems (the labour system, the tax system, the education system, spatial planning, etc.). A promising set of measures can be grouped as 'communication substitutes' (OECD 2001) such as teleworking, teleconferences, electronic commerce and distance learning, which use ICT within other societal systems or regimes to substitute the need for physical displacement.

For the reduction of real mobility *needs*, negative price incentives cannot be easily justified from a political point of view. For the reduction of *wants*, a financial charge can be justified more easily and also contributes to overall improvement by the creation of positive rebound effects. In general, societal acceptance of charges can be increased by using the income generated for making improvements to the mobility system itself.

In our opinion this first strategy has much untapped potential, provides relatively new opportunities and definitely needs to be given much more priority in the future. It addresses the existing rebound effect where environmental improvements at the micro level (global warming per kilometre mobility) are surpassed by increasing consumption levels at the macro level. It is not the easiest strategy because of its necessary influence on other (tax, planning, labour, etc.) policy areas. Radical examples of new planning principles can be seen in Curitiba (with an early planning decision to ensure the dominance of public transport) in Brazil 40 years ago, and in Floridsdorf (a neighbourhood accessible only to car-free persons) in Austria 10 years ago.

11.2.2.2 Promoting the use of the most sustainable modes: 'modal shift'

The promotion of the use of the most sustainable modes—a 'modal shift'—is the eternal battle to make users shift from individual private transport to collective (public) transport, from motorised to human-powered modes, from air transport to rail transport

Overall vision
To get people voluntarily shifting to the more sustainable modes needs clear and significant advantages offered by the alternatives in terms of time, comfort, costs and image. Success stories with increased market share can be found such as the example of high-speed trains connecting Brussels with Paris and London. For cost arguments to count in practice for users, a more balanced perception or reality of costs is needed across the modes, probably all expressed in comparable variable costs. It is an illusion to try to make large numbers of the population abandon their cars without contextual changes; the goal should be to support a reconsidering of the choice of mobility mode depending on the purpose of the trip. In the urban environment the potential is great for this strategy; in rural environments this strategy is much more limited, as these areas suffer from a larger private–public transport gap. From Chapter 7 we can also conclude that many people moving from the countryside to the city are already willing to give up their (second) car, showing that people are able to adapt to contextual changes. In recent years it has been encouraging to see how the level of urban governance has grown in importance and taken on responsibility to improve local mobility systems. A radical idea that was discussed at the third workshop

concerned a new business model for cars that could make the fixed and variable costs comparison with public transport more balanced.

11.2.2.3 Improving the sustainability performance of all modes

Overall vision

As all motorised mobility modes are among the largest environmentally polluting activities per unit of time, and as transport in general is such a large contributor to societal pollution, producers and consumers have to make significant improvements. At present, the responsibility of producers is much more explicitly regulated than the responsibility of consumers. For polluting emissions (CO, NO_x, SO_2, VOCs, lead) the technological improvements have been impressive, and absolute decoupling has been achieved, such that lower total emission levels have been achieved despite growth in consumption levels. For CO_2 no decoupling has been achieved at all and progress is too slow, partly because of buying and use behaviour, and partly because of slow technological progress. Stronger stimuli for much more intense sustainable innovation efforts and also public market support (GPP, tax policy) during first market confrontation are needed. But this strategy also includes changes in the way lease cars are taxed. It is not clear yet whether sustainable innovations are to be expected more from new entrants or from the existing automotive industry (Wells 2008). A promising approach that simultaneously addresses the three main sustainability problems of car transport (congestion, CO_2 and casualties) is the 'intelligent transport system'. The combination of telematics and ICT holds great potential for better managing travel demand (OECD 2001).

Introduction of biofuels is relatively easy from a system perspective as the infrastructure and technology needs only minor changes (although Euro 4/Euro 5 diesel engines do not allow for high percentages of biodiesel).

Hybridisation of cars can be considered a technologically intermediate step towards electric and hydrogen fuel cell vehicles. For the hydrogen society to become a reality significant changes are needed, including a sustainable way of producing hydrogen, which will require new demands for infrastructure, competing for land with other societal demands. Also, substantial technological challenges still exist for hydrogen transportation infrastructure and for the storage of hydrogen on board a car.

The nearest step forward might be created by niche markets for small electric cars in urban or densely populated areas. Producers are already investing in this, and several cities and regions (Israel, Denmark, Australia, and also Paris as a follow-up to the bike rental scheme) are planning to build the necessary battery recharging infrastructure (Betterplace 2008).[1]

1 Go to the Betterplace website, www.betterplace.com, accessed 17 March 2009.

Pressure on the air transport system to act is growing strongly at present, at the same pace as its strong growth. The legal governance aspects for international air transport and tough international competition complicate the introduction of measures: only a truly coordinated international effort on 'a level playing field' will work. Part of this strategy is the contribution that biofuels can make in producing renewable energy. Currently, there is a strong debate going on about the sustainability of the so-called first-generation biofuels as they are competing for land with other basic needs (food). The second-generation biofuels, intended to reduce these tensions, are based on using waste-streams as input for biofuel, but these still need more technological progress for implementation.

Figure 11.1 shows how these three strategies relate to the mobility and wider transport system itself and also to other societal systems. This figure also shows how the transport of goods shares much of the same (road) infrastructure with the mobility system, leading to additional congestion. Many measures are aimed at reducing congestion on the roads from the growing transport system, such as: trucks not being allowed to overtake during peak hours, high charges (£200) for trucks wanting to deliver in the centre of London during the daytime, other labour hours in harbours for logistical handling to better spread the pressure on roads and so on. Evidently, these measures also often require changes in other societal systems (such as in the labour regime, requiring discussion about working hours).

Box 11.4 Statements about visions

- Within the regulatory framework it has been possible to introduce limits to the composition of fuels, limits to emissions per kilometre, limits on the noise level of aeroplanes, limits on access to certain parts of the infrastructure and so on, but limits to consumption are not to be expected within a free-market economy

- The common understanding that it is the sole responsibility of the public service and a public task to develop sufficient mobility infrastructure complicates the finding of solutions to sustainability because, at the same time, the use of mobility systems is a free-market concept

- It is not sufficient to analyse lifestyles and niche differences among consumers in order to achieve system changes

- Leisure time mobility and holiday travel are of growing importance to the developments in the mobility systems

- Only households in high-density urban environments can do the same as the Dutch writer Harry Mulisch: 'I got rid of the car, when I want to drive I have to stand still, when I want to stand still (to park) I have to drive a lot' ('t Hart 2006)

FIGURE 11.1   Strategies for sustainable mobility within mobility and other societal systems

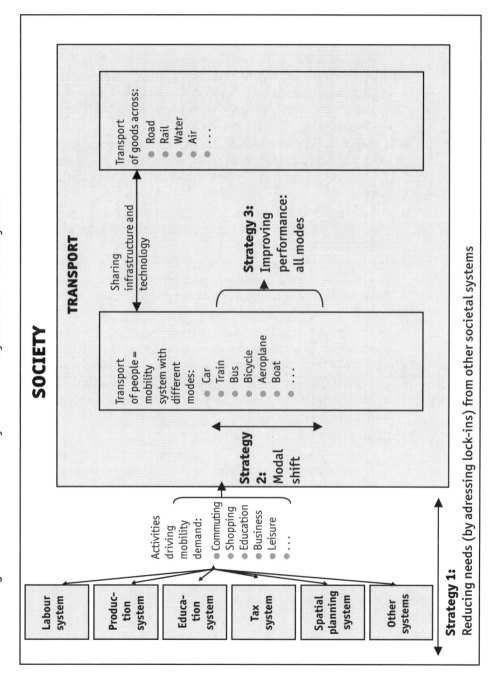

- For a change towards more sustainable (mobility) behaviour one usually needs interest, time and sometimes money; if one of these is lacking, it will not happen. Price incentives to promote more sustainable mobility behaviour need to be intense in order to change: 'no pain, no change'
- Policy efforts for sustainable production and consumption patterns within mobility inevitably must be policy mixes combining different policy instruments, addressing simultaneously both the consumption side and the production side of the mobility system
- It is more realistic, on the whole, to make car use more sustainable, rather than force people into other modes. People are not going to abandon their cars willingly, so it is best to make the cars themselves sustainable
- In many situations, personal and private human-power modes may well offer a more attractive alternative to motorised personal mobility than public modes
- Any successful attempt to change travelling and travel mode choices is based on accepting that (perceived) autonomy is a basic human need and that efficient mobility is central to a well-functioning society
- In long-distance trips the aeroplane is not such a bad environmental choice compared with, for instance, travelling alone by car; more worrying is the fact that aeroplanes allow us to travel further in shorter time-frames and as such lead to increased emissions per unit of time
- Behavioural campaigns for car pooling and car sharing in general had and will have limited success; humans' sense of freedom seems more important than economic savings
- Fundamental solutions are based on:
    - Use scarcity as a control strategy (time, money, space, facilities)
    - Appropriate pricing of behaviour that is attractive to consumers but has a high impact; and stimulation of alternatives with low impact
    - Always considering potential feedback mechanisms between supply and demand for all transport modes (including the soft modes!)

11.2.3 Sustainable consumption and production in the domain: from experiments to niches to mainstream

An experiment might be defined as a kind of large-scale pilot-test to learn something about new technology, the behaviour of the consumer or the use of new infrastructure without the intention of being economically profitable from the start.

Usually, a niche is a relatively small part of the market where the chances for market success are more favourable because of the specific context of the niche market and where part of the intention is to understand and create market success and profitability. The fact that a case is located in just one of Europe's cities is not decisive in being a niche but is interesting for the scaling-up potential to other cities or the mainstream.

A mainstream action could be defined as a new product or service solution intended to compete in the full conventional market. So, the conclusion is that this classification is most related to intention and to a lesser extent to the scale of market confrontation.

TABLE 11.1 Classification of case descriptions

Case description	Experiment, niche or mainstream?
Chapter 3: Work Closer to Home, The Netherlands	Experiment
Chapter 4: Carbon compensation scheme for air mobility, Norway	Niche
Chapter 5: Madrid's high-occupancy vehicle lanes	Niche and mainstream
Chapter 6: Appeals to promote consumer responsibility, Copenhagen	Experiment
Chapter 7: Breaking car-use habit (residential relocation), Munich	Niche
Chapter 8: Congestion charge scheme, London	Mainstream
Chapter 9: Consumer-oriented strategies in new car purchasing, The Netherlands	Mainstream
Chapter 10: Environmental vehicle excise duty, Sweden	Mainstream

From the two experiments (Chapters 3 and 6), we have learned two lessons regarding human mobility behaviour:

- The importance of value–norm development and promotion
- The need to solve user lock-in situations

From the niches (Chapters 4, 5 and 7) we have learned several lessons:

● Authorities should themselves set the right example if they want others to take voluntary action

● For public transport to be an attractive alternative to the personal car the time advantage is decisive as is the apparent difficulty of making people willing to use car pooling with non-family members and non-colleagues

● Information campaigns, free help-desks and free trials meet with more success when offered at the right moment in a person's life, particularly at key life decisions

● All the niches offer good scaling-up potential

From the mainstream cases (Chapters 5, 8, 9 and 10) we have learned several lessons:

● The importance of an integrated policy with coherent incentives at several points in the system

● The limited effect on consumers of information; the effect of tax reduction measures to encourage sustainable behaviour

● The importance of a vision and a 'product champion'

To our knowledge none of these mainstream cases was preceded by previous niches before scaling up. They were designed more or less directly for a mainstream application, sometimes inspired by foreign mainstream examples. Not all SCP improvements will follow the route of experiment through niche to mainstream. Some might jump directly from experiment to mainstream, from foreign mainstream or from idea to mainstream: 'There are many roads leading to Rome.'

For a very big system change such as to a hydrogen economy the steps from experiment to niche to mainstream make much more sense. First, technological tests are needed and are currently on the way. The first probably protected niche market will be the bus application. A bus has enough space for the larger fuel tank, and a simplified central fuel infrastructure will be sufficient as buses return to their home base several times per day. For mainstream applications an enormous system change—a full hydrogen fuel infrastructure—would be needed right from the start.

11.3 A short comparison with the food and housing domains

The SCORE! project has also provided analyses of two other priority consumption domains: food, and housing and energy use. The results of this work have been published in two other books in the 'System Innovation for Sustainability' series (Tischner *et al.* 2009; Lahlou *et al.* 2010). This section gives a short comparison of the main differences and similarities across domains, using some key concepts introduced in the first SCORE! book (Tukker *et al.* 2008) and elaborated in Chapter 2 and the conclusions presented in this chapter. It concerns:

- Characteristics of the system: is there agreement on the sense of urgency of change, the means to realise change and the key players in the system that may drive change?

- Potential role of each actor in the 'triangle of change': what can consumers, producers and governments do?

- What factors contribute to windows of opportunity for change and what are the main challenges?

Table 11.2 presents this comparison, summarising information from Chapter 2 and the concluding chapter of each book. We see from this that we must treat each differently rather than focusing on common strategies applicable to each domain, as the three fields have different characteristics.

When it comes down to agreement on the sense of urgency and the means of realising change, the food area appears to be complicated. Some would pursue organic and local food production, whereas others point at the fact that precision-farmed food produced at the place where local conditions are optimal can be sustainable given the relatively low impact of (e.g. ship) transport. Genetically modified organisms (GMOs) are extremely controversial, being seen as a means of enhancing food production sustainably by some, and seen as fully unnatural by others. The sense of urgency in the areas of mobility (energy use, congestion) and housing (energy use) are much more widely shared; here, the only dispute is to what extent one can pursue an outright reduction of mobility or housing area needs. The housing area is also the domain where a clear direction for solving problems seems clear (energy-neutral housing), whereas in mobility there is a need for more convergence of insight into what will work.

When it comes down to the potential role of actors in the triangle of change (an issue that will be elaborated on in the mobility domain in the next section), one sees important differences too. Unlike in the case of mobility and housing and energy-using products, in the food area consumers have a relatively high degree of freedom of consumer choice.[2] Although they are obviously constrained

---

2 In the area of housing and energy use consumers in most EU countries now also have a free choice of energy suppliers, but the practical hurdles in this field still seem significant.

TABLE 11.2 Comparison between food, mobility and housing of system characteristics and potential role of players

The system	Food		Mobility		Housing	
	Score	Comment	Score	Comment	Score	Comment
Agreement on goals and sense of urgency	Low	There is no consensus on what a sustainable food system should look like. There is dispute about the sustainability benefit of genetically modified organisms (GMOs) compared with regular food, organic compared with precision-farmed food, and locally grown compared with imported food	Medium	Reducing congestion, CO_2 emissions and emissions of other pollutants are generally accepted goals. The need for an absolute reduction of mobility is much less so	High	Zero-energy houses and low-energy-using products are generally accepted goals. Limiting the housing area per person to reduce energy use is not, however, feasible
Certainty or agreement about means	Low	See above	Low	Few success stories of change; the growth of mobility demand seems unstoppable	Medium	Many successful illustrative projects on zero-energy houses are available, but mainstreaming seems difficult
Geographical characteristics	Global	Most modern food chains span the globe	Global and local	There is just a handful of car manufacturers left. The local situation, however, significantly determines mobility patterns and availability of alternatives	Local	The building industry is rather locally organised and has local characteristics
Power nodes in the system		Retailers, major food companies		Car producers, infrastructure providers		Varies per country: social housing agencies, landowners, developers or customers

The triangle of change	Food		Mobility		Housing	
	Score	Comment	Score	Comment	Score	Comment
Potential for consumer-driven change	Medium	Consumers make daily purchase choices and can change diets, though in practice they are locked in by routines, habits and availability of food alternatives	Low	Consumers have often limited choice with regard to their pattern and means of mobility, except during holidays	Low	In most countries consumers have little power over how houses are built
Potential for producer-driven change	Medium to high	Retailers (e.g. by choice editing), major food companies (e.g. via certification schemes such as the MSC (Marine Stewardship Council) and smaller companies (e.g. Bionade) all have proven to be able to drive change	Low to medium	Automotive companies at best will realise incremental change; alternative mobility providers tend to stay in niches	Medium	Many illustrative projects are available, but mainstreaming seems difficult
Potential for government-driven change	Medium	Government can support change by public procurement and regulation, but the latter will work mainly to set minimum standards rather than by driving radical change	Medium to high	Government has a major role to play in spatial planning, the availability of public transport and in encouraging a more sustainable modal split	Medium	Via energy labelling and minimum standards governments can ensure basic energy performance, but radical change is possible only if zero-energy housing is mainstreamed
Factors providing windows of opportunity		Consumer expectations about health, safety and social issues reformulated the Common Agricultural Policy (CAP)		High energy prices, congestion		High energy prices
Main challenges		Negotiating a view on sustainable food and implementing this. Various views and related production structures may co-exist		Overcoming various lock-ins (regional planning, physical infrastructure, the importance of the car industry to many industrialised countries)		Mainstreaming of proven practices with regard to low-energy houses; dealing with the existing housing stock

by habits, routine and so on they can rather easily switch food choices and even diets in rather radical ways. Such choices can be made on an almost daily basis, whereas for mobility and housing the physical lock-ins are reduce consumer choice significantly. Compared with the building sector, it seems that the power at the production side in the domains of mobility (car and infrastructure provision) and food (retailers, major food producers) is probably much more concentrated. Interestingly, in the food area one sees that such mainstream players seem more active in pursuing sustainability goals and related management systems than in the car industry, most probably because of the greater flexibility and implicit consumer expectations with regard to environmental and social responsibility. The driving forces, main challenges and the role of government seems rather different in each domain too.

- In the building area the main challenge seems to be to mainstream solutions, focusing on realising zero-energy houses. For new houses, this implies the mainstreaming of proven solutions, whereas for existing housing stock of question how to tackle the problem is still not solved. A smart innovation and diffusion policy seems the main challenge here

- In the food area, one sees an implicit societal negotiation going on about what implies 'sustainable food'. There seems to be, however, a relatively high flexibility in the food system and a supportive role from government may be sufficient

- In the mobility area, the problems and lock-ins seem most problematic. Given the important role of infrastructure, spatial planning, the need to provide alternative modes of transport and the fact that the few success stories rely heavily on government incentives (e.g. see Chapter 8), a strong integral role for government seems inevitable

11.4 Actions by actor group and time-horizon

The triangle of change consists of government, business and consumers. Particularly in the case of mobility, 'government' has a pluralistic meaning and role. Different levels of government are active (international, national, regional, local) and also several (semi-)public bodies exist in the operation of mobility systems. For business the same is true, as there exists a wide array of businesses active in the mobility system, constructing infrastructure, producing and selling vehicles, providing maintenance and mobility services and so on.

Box 11.5 Statements about actions

- In order to reduce commuter traffic a tax credit should be given to those who move closer to their place of work
- Infrastructure (city design) should be compact, and oriented towards transit and human-powered in order to encourage the use of public transport, biking and walking and to avoid car traffic
- Inner cities should be closed off to anything but zero-emission vehicles
- Attracting people into alternatives is more feasible in a free-market economy than is forcing them to do so
- Sustainable mobility can be achieved only through a combination of a number of instruments and interventions:
  - Adapt conditions so that they favour sustainable forms of mobility and reduce wasteful mobility to a minimum, combined with technical improvements for all types of non-human-powered forms of mobility
    - Through city and other types of planning (a) reduce the need for motorised mobility and (b) make mass public transport relatively more attractive than individual motorised mobility
    - Remove 'perverse subsidies' to unsustainable forms of mobility and in general develop the price structure in the mobility area so that relative prices reflect total social (including environmental) costs
  - Use taxing in a way that avoids or reduces consumer over-investments in motorised means of transportation
  - Use communication and social marketing to
    - Produce voter acceptance
    - Change consumer habits away from unnecessary use of motorised transport
- Measures for increasing the safety level of the driver and passengers should no longer lead to much higher car weights; it is time to maximise behavioural change
- Car-sharing services should be subsidised and widely available

11.4.1 Short term: means and ends not very controversial

Most of the actions listed in Table 11.3, from cases and desktop research (EEA 2008a), can be located within the mobility system; some are located in other societal systems and regimes.

TABLE 11.3 Actions and leading actors, by regime

Landscape (factors out of reach for actors in the regime)

- Meta-structures: infrastructure, geopolitical facts and so on
- Meta-values: individual sovereignty, democracy, free markets and trade, growth, fairness
- Meta-trends: individualisation, internationalisation, intensification, informatisation
- Meta-shocks: wars, crises, natural disasters

Regime: Production ⟷ Markets ⟷ Consumption

Production regime	Markets regime	Consumption regime
Business	*Government*	Consumers, citizens, non-governmental organisations
• Invest more in sustainable incremental and radical innovation	• Internalising externalities, through taxes also for aviation	• Exercise sustainable choice
• Intensify experiments that address several unsustainable issues at the same time (e.g. intelligent transport systems)	• Avoid or reduce lock-in situations from other policies that in practice enhance need for mobility	• Take steps towards lifestyles of health and sustainability (LOHAS)
• Start from a long-term vision	• Promote balanced cost models across private and public transport through charging, subsidising and lower VAT rates for energy-efficient vehicles	• As citizen and worker: articulate and encourage sustainable meta-values
• Investigate new alliances for new sustainable business	• Promote transparency on social and environmental issues related to products	• Reinvestigate own mobility patterns from time to time with an open mind
• Promote industry self-regulation on the above (although the ACEA covenant failed; Section 11.1.3)	• Create budgetary-neutral tax incentives or reinvest environmental taxes and excise into the mobility system	• Use a balanced cost model
	• Use the many 'buttons' authorities have in a coherent way	

Production regime	Markets regime	Consumption regime
Government ● Provide level playing field supporting the above (covenants, regulations, standards) ● Foster green innovation systems and support sustainable (niche) entrepreneurs ● Articulate and encourage sustainable meta-values		*Government* (combine the below for effect!) ● GPP to include employee mobility plans ● Provide alternatives for sustainable choice of similar quality ● Spatial planning to include long-term mobility planning ● Create no-need contexts ● Motivate via appealing engagement and leadership. ● Promote positive attitude for more sustainable norms and values ● Invest in social innovation ● Provide better consumption statistics to better monitor the drivers for needs and wants *Business* ● Promote sustainable consumer feedback (e.g. economy meters) ● Apply sustainability marketing and demand-side management ● Have employee mobility plans

11.4.2 Medium term: agreement on direction of change; means uncertain

In the medium to long term, a reorientation of infrastructure development in the direction of sustainable mobility is of central importance. This implies a change from the 'more-transport-is-good-transport' perspective, prevailing in many places today, to a more detailed and elaborate perspective that integrates the different economic, environmental and social dimensions of sustainability. Moreover, it implies addressing both the direct and indirect implications of new infrastructure developments from a long-term perspective. In land-use planning the debate persists on whether the compact-city concept is better for mobility than a decentralised concentration of cities (Holden 2007) as one has to take into account commuting, shopping and leisure mobility.

This also means a renewed discussion of the connections between infrastructure and consumption patterns. To a stronger degree than before it is important to understand the role of infrastructure as a creator of transport and mobility needs, not just as an answer to existing demands.

Governments have in some cases begun to take up this challenge, among other things, through the overall notion of 'sustainable mobility' (instead of transport policy) and 'mobility that creates real value' (instead of just mobility); however, much more work needs to be done (Gudmundsson 2005).

Further improvement of public transport systems is obviously an important element in connection with the re-orientation of infrastructure development. A relatively higher prioritisation of public transport infrastructure is needed, especially in urban areas and between cities.

Compared with other areas of consumption, such as that relating to food, consumers in the mobility area are much dependent on established systems. In many cases they feel they have little choice concerning, say, mode of transport to work. (The picture is different when it comes to leisure-time mobility and holidays.) Nevertheless, despite lock-in in mainstream consumption patterns, there are people 'doing it differently' and minorities that have shaped their lifestyles and practices in agreement with alternative patterns of mobility consumption.

From the medium-term perspective, there are two particular aspects that are important in this connection. First, there is a need to maintain awareness and share information about the variety of means of consumption that exists. Second, there is a need to establish organisations that can gather together consumers and their experiences and work for improved opportunities for sustainable mobility. The two aspects can often overlap. In many cases the media will also be an important actor in this connection. Example of such consumer organisations are the associations of 'green motorists' that have appeared in some countries, organising people that, on the one hand, are concerned about the sustainability impacts of car transport and want changes made but, on the other hand, use cars for a larger or smaller part of their transport.

The niches of more or less alternative ways of consumption can be productive for business actors and developers working on the production side of the mobility system. The consumers can be seen as lead users, providing ideas and showing ways for development. To establish arenas of development where interaction between users and developers can take place over a period of time can be of central importance for the development of new mobility opportunities in a broader market. Consumer organisations, business actors and policy actors can be active in establishing such arenas (Valderrama and Jørgensen 2008).

Apart from mobility policy and transport policy, developments in industry policy will also be important for the contribution of business to sustainable mobility in the medium term. Industry policy traditionally has not addressed sustainability issues. This is, however, starting to change. In countries such as Germany and France government actors are working on developing ecological industry policies. Innovation and technology for sustainable mobility make up one of the highest-prioritised areas here. Eco-innovation is another concept used by governments and, for example, by the European Commission, for innovation and industry-oriented policy efforts for sustainability.

The background to these strategic developments is the recognition of the necessity of handling the radical current changes in the global economy and ecology in an integrated manner. Moreover, the markets for environmentally friendly technologies are growing fast and they are expected to become central to the world economy in the future. Considerable employment and export opportunities will appear in these fields and the eco-oriented industries will become relatively more influential in society than they are today. They will not be small or minor industries.

For the area of sustainable mobility, it will be of central importance how, and whether, these policies can support a qualified interplay between the consumption side and the production side of the mobility area.

For the medium- to long-term perspective, a build-up of 'systemic reflexivity' for learning on sustainable mobility is important (Thomsen *et al.* 2005). A well-functioning monitoring system is a central element in this. This includes development of a fuller set of indicators for sustainability and mobility than exists today. The systemic reflexivity will also need to include more qualitative analyses in order to ensure continuous discussion and learning on the issue.

An important part of the systemic reflexivity for learning on sustainable mobility is taking place in public institutions and it is important that reflexivity practice is integrated in the institutions and in the mutual communication and interaction between institutions (see the discussion on institutional reflexivity in Wynne 1993). Systemic reflexivity in institutions provides a basis for broader dialogues and discussions in society about mobility and sustainability.

11.4.3 Long term: controversy over means and ends

Within the mobility system there still exists no consensus about the best means of addressing the global warming effects of mobility; therefore several means have been developed in parallel, such as the use of biofuels for road and air transport, renewable electricity production for trains, hybrid cars, hydrogen fuel cell cars—all requiring technological (and sometimes big system) changes. Recently, the design of a so-called Personal Air and Land Vehicle (PAL-V) was published, allowing one to fly over congested roads if needed. It is a combination of a carver (three-wheel motor) and a gyrocopter and has two seats. This solves congestion problems for the owner, but what will large-scale introduction mean for traffic safety and total emissions?

Debate and research on best land-use planning is still going on (Holden 2007) as people living in larger, higher-density, cities need less energy for daily commuting but also seem to need much more energy for leisure travel. Research from India showed that RUrban design of Goa city including consolidation into 13 settlements would allow for an urban space without cars, both at low cost and with lowest ecological footprint (Revi 2006); is this also valid for Europe and how can this be implemented this in a socially acceptable way?

Fundamental will be how the needs and wants for mobility develop in the world society as a whole and whether we can allow 'the sky as a limit' or have to move to tradable permits at a personal level. Countries and continents have been making transitions at different rates from hunter-gatherer societies, to agricultural societies, to industrial societies, towards service industry societies . . . globalising . . . informatising . . . (what will come next?) . . . societies. The development of sustainable mobility is deeply integrated with international development issues and differences between economically richer and poorer parts of the world. To deal with long-term perspectives of SCP patterns in the mobility area implies a significant degree of international communication and negotiation. The international agreements that are established on the issue will need to be developed further and extended significantly.

Whether it is possible to combine environmental sustainability and economic growth in the long run is a question that will be discussed much more in the future and not only in the mobility area. For some decades it has been an accepted view that economic development would not fundamentally threaten the environment; however, serious climate problems and security of supply issues have drawn renewed attention to the possibility of limits to growth. Despite a partial decoupling in some fields of economic development, stronger efforts are needed.

In the short and medium term there is no doubt that, with a lot more creativity, innovation and an integrated approach, a better balance between economic growth and environmental performance can be achieved. In the long term it will be necessary to develop new models of society much less dependent on mobility.

11.5 Conclusions

Mobility has three main sustainability issues: CO_2 emissions from cars and air transport, congestion and casualties due to road traffic. Sustainable mobility innovations usually bring about changes across one two or three of the main system elements: infrastructure, vehicles, behaviour.

The four main players in the sociotechnical regime are authorities, vehicle producers, users and fuel producers. They are tightly connected to the system elements but authorities have the most intertwined role in the system as a provider and owner of road and public transport infrastructure, as an operator of public transport services (although privatisation is starting up), as a regulator for safety, traffic rules, product standards and so on, as a cashier for the fuel, vehicle and road taxes and excises and as a public procurer of mobility. This large number of 'buttons' creates enormous opportunities to exert influence but also requires coordinated efforts to show effect.

There are three main strategies for more sustainable mobility:

● Reducing the need for mobility

● Promoting the use of the most sustainable modes: 'modal shift'

● Improving the sustainability performance of all modes

The first strategy requires much more attention and has much untapped potential. Efforts in the short term should be focused on reducing the need for mobility by solving the existing professional, social and economic lock-in situations that users and consumers are confronted with by addressing other policy areas such as tax, planning and labour policy, which, in fact, are part of other societal systems. In the long term it requires a new societal system much less dependent on motorised mobility.

The second and third strategies should be intensified, as all mobility modes will continue to exist for many years to come because of the high inertia in infrastructure (both for mobility and because of the built infrastructure).

References

De Graaff, T., and A. van Leuvensteijn (2007) *The Impact of Housing Market Institutions on Labour Mobility* (Centraal Planbureau [CPB] Discussion Paper 82; The Hague: CPB, June 2007).

EEA (European Environment Agency) (2008a) *Time for Action : Towards Sustainable Consumption and Production in Europe* (Copenhagen: EEA).

—— (2008b) *Success Stories within the Road Transport Sector on Reducing Greenhouse Gas Emissions and Producing Ancillary Benefits* (Copenhagen: EEA).

EU (2006) 'Commission presents the outstanding results of the CUTE project and announces new action for Clean Public Transport', press release; europa.eu/rapid/pressReleasesAction. do?reference=IP/06/604, accessed 3 September 2009.

Gudmundsson, H. (2005) 'Mobility as Policy Concept', in T.U. Thomsen, L.D. Nielsen and H. Gudmundsson (eds.), *Social Perspectives on Mobility* (Aldershot, UK: Ashgate): 107-26.

't Hart, M. (2006) 'De OV-fiets', *NRC Handelsblad*, 4 October 2006.

Holden, E. (2007) *Achieving Sustainable Mobility: Everyday and Leisure-time Travel in the EU* (Aldershot, UK: Ashgate).

Hoogma, R., R. Kemp, J. Schot and B. Truffer (2002) *Experimenting for Sustainable Transport: The Approach of Strategic Niche Management* (London: E & FN Spon).

Lahlou, S., M. Charter and T. Woolman (eds.) (2010) *System Innovation for Sustainability 4: Case Studies in Sustainable Consumption and Production—Housing/Energy-Using Products* (Sheffield, UK: Greenleaf Publishing, forthcoming).

OECD (Organisation for Economic Cooperation and Development) (2001) 'Influencing Road Travel Demand: You Can't Reach Kyoto By Car'; www.stockholm.snf.se/urtidarleden/ Influencing.doc, accessed 17 March 2009.

Revi, A., S. Prakash, R. Mehrotra, G. Bhat, K. Gupta and R. Gore (2006) 'Goa 2100: The Transition to a Sustainable RUrban Design', *Environment and Urbanization* 18.1: 51-65.

Thomsen, T.U., L.D. Nielsen and H. Gudmundsson (2005) *Social Perspectives on Mobility* (Aldershot, UK: Ashgate).

Tischner, U., E. Stø, U. Kjærnes and A. Tukker (eds.) (2009) *System Innovation for Sustainability 3: Case Studies in Sustainable Consumption and Production—Food and Agriculture* (Sheffield, UK: Greenleaf Publishing, forthcoming).

Tukker, A., M. Charter, C. Vezzoli, E. Stø and M. Munch Andersen (eds.) (2008) *System Innovation for Sustainability 1: Perspectives on Radical Change to Sustainable Consumption and Production* (Sheffield, UK: Greenleaf Publishing).

Valderrama, A., and U. Jørgensen (2008) 'Urban Transport Systems in Bogotá and Copenhagen: An Approach from STS', *Built Environment* 34.2: 200-17.

Van den Bergh, J., E. van Leeuwen, F. Oosterhuis, P. Rietveld and E. Verhoef (2007) 'Social Learning by Doing in Sustainable Transport Innovations: Ex-post Analysis of Common Factors behind Successes and Failures', *Research Policy* 36.2: 247-59.

Wells, P. (2008) 'Alternative Business Models for a Sustainable Automotive Industry', in A. Tukker, M. Charter, C.Vezzoli, E. Stø and M. Munch Andersen (eds.), *System Innovation for Sustainability 1: Perspectives on Radical Change to Sustainable Consumption and Production* (Sheffield, UK: Greenleaf Publishing): 80-98.

Wynne, B. (1993) 'Public Uptake of Science: A Case For Institutional Reflexivity', *Public Understanding of Science* 2: 321-37.

About the contributors

Sebastian Bamberg is professor of Social Psychology and Methods at the University of Applied Science Bielefeld, Germany. His research involves the development and evaluation of theory-driven intervention programmes aiming to change environmentally harmful behaviours, especially car use. At a theoretical level, he is interested in modelling the environmental, social and psychological determinants of behavioural change. Recent projects have included laboratory experiments on the interplay of values, responsibility attribution and emotions and the desire to change environmentally harmful behaviours, the correlational test of stage-based models of behavioural change, and three large field studies evaluating the behavioural impact of theory-based social marketing campaigns.

Mads Borup is a senior scientist in the Innovation Systems and Foresight section at the Technical University of Denmark's Department for Management Engineering. His areas of work are systems of innovation, governance of innovation and sociotechnical change processes in the fields of eco-innovation and energy innovation. An important part of his work is strategy processes and foresight on environment and technology. Mads has experience of numerous Danish and international research projects as well as performing in an advisory capacity to policy- and decision-makers on these issues.

Mr **J.W.A. (Arjan) Dekker** is co-owner of Adapt BV, a company focusing on sustainable solutions for environmental issues via internet or internet-related media. Adapt BV is currently developing a new mobility platform in cooperation with the city of The Hague, The Netherlands, the Ministry of Transport and TFMM (Task Force Mobility Management). Arjan Dekker originally has a financial background and used to be account manager for exports and treasurer for an international company until 2004. At the beginning of 2005, together with a business partner, he founded Adapt BV, in which the activities for the website WERKdichterbijhuis.nl are legally based. Since 2008 Dekker has also been working as a consultant for Adequaat in the field of marketing and communications.

Theo Geerken is Project Manager for the Product and Technology Studies group which forms part of the Transition Energy and Environment Unit at the Flemish Research Institute VITO. This group focuses on research for both industry and government by applying methods and concepts such as LCA, Eco-design, Substance Flow Analysis, Cleaner Production, Sustainability Evaluation, Environmentally Extended Input–Output Modelling and Technology Assessment. Theo is a civil engineer in physics. He has industry experience in the reprographic sector consisting of 16 years in research, product development and engineering and integrating environmental goals into business practice. He has worked at VITO since 2000 and was WP leader for Mobility within the SCORE! project.

Since 2007, Mrs **Simone J.F.M. Maase** has been a consultant in social and sustainable entrepreneurship at a Dutch association GreenWish. GreenWish focuses on the realisation of small social and sustainable initiatives in society. It provides information, coaching and training, and offers its network to private clients who want to develop their sustainable or social project. Simone is an industrial design engineer. For the past 11 years she has been working as a product developer, researcher and consultant. Currently she is working on her PhD thesis on the establishment of partnerships between social entrepreneurs and the business sector.

Mr **Jorrit Nijhuis** is an environmental scientist who has worked as a PhD researcher (since 2005) at the Environmental Policy Group at Wageningen University, The Netherlands. This group is active in the field of environmental social science and policy research. Jorrit is part of a research programme on sustainable lifestyles and consumption patterns which is part-financed by the Knowledge network on System Innovations (KSI). He is currently finalising his thesis on the active involvement of citizen-consumers in transition processes to sustainable mobility. In addition, since 2009 he has been working at the Directorate-General for Public Works and Water Management (Rijkswaterstaat) of the Ministry of Transport.

John Thøgersen is Professor of Economic Psychology at the Aarhus School of Business, Aarhus University, Denmark. He heads the Marketing and Sustainability Research Group at the Department of Marketing and Statistics at the Aarhus School of Business. His current research includes projects on social norms in the environmental field, promoting energy conservation in households, and intergenerational transfer of environmental concerns. He has published extensively on consumption and environment issues in refereed journals such as the *Journal of Economic Psychology, International Journal of Research in Marketing, Psychology and Marketing, European Journal of Marketing, Basic and Applied Social Psychology, Journal of Environmental Psychology, Environment and Behavior* and *Business Strategy and the Environment*. John is editor of the *Journal of Consumer Policy*, published by Springer.

Dr **Arnold Tukker** joined TNO in 1990 after some time working for the Dutch Environment Ministry. Over time, his focus shifted from life-cycle assessment, material flow analysis and risk assessment to interactive policy-making and sustainable system innovation and transition management. In 1998 he published a book on societal disputes on toxic substances, for which he was awarded a PhD from Tilburg University. He has published about 40 peer-reviewed papers, 5 books, 10 book chapters and 150 other publications, and is frequently asked as invited speaker worldwide. In his career, he has been awarded over €15 million in mainly international research grants. He currently manages the research programme on Transitions and System Innovation within TNO Built Environment and Geosciences, Business Unit Innovation and Environment. This programme was evaluated as one of TNO's top-ranking programmes during the 2006 scientific assessment exercise. Arnold is the initiator and manager of the SCORE! network.

Sander van den Burg was appointed as a postdoctoral researcher at the Environmental Policy Group, Wageningen University, The Netherlands, between 2006 and 2008. His research focused on the emergence of new arrangements for environmental governance, with an emphasis on the changes in sustainable consumption policies. These were studied under the Contrast research project. His PhD research, completed in 2006, focused on the changing role of information in environmental politics and featured case studies on energy monitoring, labelling and disclosure. Since 2008 Sander has worked as consultant for DGMR (www.dgmr.nl), advising government and corporations on sustainable urban and industrial development.

An Vercalsteren graduated in 1994 as engineer in electromechanics. Since 1996 she has been working as a member of the scientific staff at VITO where she has built up comprehensive knowledge in the field of sustainable chain management. She has been involved in the performance of different LCA, ecodesign, eco-efficiency and EE–IO projects in which widely differing product types have been analysed, with both government and industry as target groups. She has participated in various projects related to sustainable development.

Index